Driving Scenic N

A GUIDE TO TOURING NEW ZEALAND B.

C000226710

DAVE CHOWDHURY

CRAIG POTTON PUBLISHING

Dave Chowdhury is a Wellington writer and editor. In 2000 he completed a degree in international relations and political philosophy, then took the first job that came along – writing this guide. Despite assertions to the contrary, his friends remain unconvinced that spending summer travelling New Zealand constituted work.

ACKNOWLEDGEMENTS

I would like to acknowledge all at Craig Potton Publishing, especially Betzy Iannuzzi, Robbie Burton, Craig Potton, Noleen Campbell, Tina Delceg and Phillippa Duffy; and those friends and family who provided fine company and floor space in the course of my travels: Roy and Eileen Chowdhury, Kevin and Margaret O'Connor, Don and Margaret Lamont, Alison Ballance, Brendan Kane, Terry Sumner, Manfred Meyer, Irene Cahill and Gunnar Kaschka, Fred Holmes and Fi Acheson, Katherine Curran and Warren of Surat Bay Lodge, John Skilton and Suzy Ruddenklau, the Mathias Family, Steve Davies, Pat and Cheryl Sole, Marie Taylor and Richard Croad, Rob Kirkwood and Paula Marshall, John Hilhorst and Cath Gilmour, Ray and Christine Bellringer and Peter Garlick. A special thanks must go to Naomi O'Connor, my occasional assistant researcher, notetaker and coffee consultant, who made me stop at places I might otherwise have ignored.

Text: Dave Chowdhury

Production: Tina Delceg, Phillippa Duffy, Robbie Burton

Maps: Base maps supplied by Terralink Ltd; additional map work by Tina Delceg

Photography: Craig Potton

Cover Design: Jo Williams

Cover Photo: Road to Aoraki/Mt Cook by Ben Simmons

Printing: Astra Print Ltd, Wellington, NZ

Published by: Craig Potton Publishing
98 Vickerman Street, PO Box 555, Nelson, New Zealand
www.craigpotton.co.nz   info@cpp.co.nz

© 2001 Craig Potton Publishing
Reprinted 2002

ISBN 0-908802-75-7

CONTENTS

Cape Reinga

About this guide

When I was a kid growing up in the 1960s and 70s our family would load up the car – a modest Cortina in the early years, and later the ubiquitous Antipodean Holden – for long summer holidays. Being recent immigrants from the UK and India, exploring our new home gave these holidays an added impetus. New Zealand isn't that big a place and the web of roads that criss-crossed the countryside gave us access to faraway places in relatively short order. These holidays took us from our home in Taranaki to Auckland and the Far North, Rotorua, Taupo, Hawke's Bay, Wellington, and occasionally to the South Island.

Back then roads weren't as good as they are now. I remember the terrible dusty unsealed winding roads between Napier and Taupo, through the Manawatu Gorge and in the Far North. Even some of the sealed routes were tortuous winding affairs through the North Island hinterland.

Since then, most of these roads have been sealed, straightened and no doubt made safer. The web of roads remains, the major difference is that there are more cars on the road than ever. That and the fact that tourism has become a major world industry, which has led to the development of a greatly expanded tourism infrastructure in New Zealand.

The other significant shift has been from the pre-arranged package tour of New Zealand to 'free and independent travel' holidays. Instead of plying the traditional tourist trade routes by bus, train or plane, tourists are travelling everywhere in hired campervans and rental vehicles, or increasingly, buying a car for the duration of their holiday, camping or staying in the many backpackers and homestays that have sprung up around the country.

This new guide is a response to this trend in tourism. In it you will find descriptions of the major touring routes in New Zealand. Highlighted are the major places of interest, tourist facilities, travel times and distances, interesting side trips, walks, campgrounds, places where you might find a good coffee or a bite to eat. I won't claim it as being an exhaustive guide, more a greatest hits if you like. What this book is not is a guide to major destinations or accommodation – instead it is about the places and landscapes that lie in-between, to be used in conjunction with your Lonely Planet, Rough Guide or AA accommodation book.

Driving in New Zealand

- **Driver licences**
  All drivers must have a current and/or an international driver licence. Vehicles are right-hand drive, and must be driven on the left-hand side of the road.

- **Safety belts**
  Wearing safety belts is compulsory for all occupants of a vehicle. Children under 5 must be restrained with an approved children's car restraint.

- **Speed limits**
  Speed limits in New Zealand are 100 km/h on the open road, and 50 km/h in built-up areas. LSZ (Limited

Speed Zones) means you must drive 50 km/h in adverse conditions (for instance poor weather) otherwise the 100 km/h limit applies. A range of limits applies at road works (30–50 km/h) and on the outskirts of urban areas (usually 70 km/h). If you're towing a trailer the limit is 80 km/h, likewise if driving a bus or truck it's 80 km/h.

■ Intersections
- Always use your indicators when turning (give 3 seconds warning before beginning the turn).
- Give way to all traffic not turning.
- Give way to all traffic crossing or approaching from your right.

■ Roundabouts
- Always turn left into a roundabout.
- Give way to all traffic on your right.
- Indicate when you are about to leave the intersection.

■ Traffic Lights
North American drivers are advised that there is no free left turn on a red traffic light.

■ Rental vehicles
Tourists over 21 years with an appropriate licence can rent virtually any type of vehicle in New Zealand – from large campervans and all terrain four-wheel-drives to small two-door hatchbacks. Prices are variable and you tend to get what you pay for. Thus at the cheaper end of the range (between $30–$40 a day, unlimited mileage) you're likely to get a vehicle which is underpowered (1500 cc or less) and unlikely to have a good or functioning stereo system – considerations if you're planning a long trip and if there's more than two of you. Choose a rental company that offers Automobile Association breakdown assistance. Hirers are responsible for maintaining oil and water levels, but if your vehicle burns oil, keep the receipts and ask to be reimbursed as it's the company's responsibility to provide you with a well-maintained vehicle. Insurance cover is usually provided, but can involve some hefty excesses ($750–$1500). Insurance won't cover broken windscreens in some cases. There are also insurance issues around unsealed roads – see next section.

■ Unsealed roads
Some routes described in this book have sections of unsealed road. For the most part these roads are well-graded and maintained, and present few difficulties when driven cautiously. New Zealanders drive these roads confidently, sometimes too confidently. But for the overseas tourists used to paved highways, gravel roads can present a serious hazard.

In one accident I came across while researching this book, two German tourists put their car 50 m down a bank above Lake Waikaremoana, having braked too hard on a corner and skidded off the road. Their vehicle stopped just metres above the water – they were extremely lucky. Unfortunately accidents involving tourists on gravel roads are commonplace, particularly on popular drives like the Catlins coast section of the Southern Scenic Route in Southland.

The best advice is to drive unsealed roads slowly – you're on holiday after all! Driving slowly gives you more control and allows a greater margin for reacting to other more confident drivers and irresponsible local drivers travelling too fast for the conditions. If you're driving an automatic, always select second or low gear to give yourself a measure of control on corners, and lessening your reliance on braking.

Secondly, if you're in a rental vehicle, check the fine print of your rental agreement because some don't insure drivers on an unsealed road, while others exclude particular roads such as any road north of Coromandel township, the last few kilometres to Cape Reinga, any mountain or skifield access road, the Skippers Gorge near Queenstown. The rental company argument that unsealed roads would be sealed if they were popular is misplaced when it comes to, for example, the last few kilometres of SH 1 to Cape Reinga. If this is an issue, renegotiate the insurance agreement, or find another rental company.

- **Slow drivers**
I thoroughly recommend slow driving, but having said that, slow drivers on New Zealand roads are a particular source of frustration for following motorists, especially on hilly or winding terrain where over-taking opportunities are limited. Campervan drivers need to be aware of this. Convenient as these vehicles are, they are also slow, cumbersome and belch smelly diesel fumes, which is annoying to anyone behind. The simple rule for the sightseeing driver is pull over at every opportunity to let others pass – it's such an easy and courteous thing to do.

- **Fuel**
Petrol and diesel are widely available, but prices vary, wildly in some cases, the further you get away from main centres or routes, or when OPEC alters production, in which case rapid falls and rises in price come with little warning. In some areas the price of fuel amounts to daylight robbery, particularly in the Far

Maori words commonly used in place names

awa – river or valley	niwa – rainbow	roa – long
hua – plenty	nui – big	roto – lake
ika – fish	pa – fortified village	rua – two
inanga – whitebait	pari – cliff	tahuna – sand dunes, beach
iti – small	pounamu – greenstone	tapu – sacred or forbidden
kai – food	puke – hill	wai – water
manga – stream or tributary	rae – cape	whanga – bay or inlet
maunga – mountain	rangi – sky	whare – house
moana – sea	repo – swamp	whenua – land or country
motu – island	rere – waterfall	

ICON KEY   🍴 Food   🚻 Toilets   ⛽ Petrol   ℹ Information

North and the South Island West Coast. My advice is to fill up at the major towns and cities where fuel is usually cheaper than the smaller localities in-between.

Visitor Information Centres, toilets, cafes
One of the greatest improvements for tourists and New Zealand travellers has been the establishment of an excellent network of visitor information centres. These will be found at all major centres and tourist destinations, usually well signposted from the main roads. Clean toilets will be found at most places, large or small. Another step forward has been the rising standard of cafés outside of the cities catering for travellers. While food is generally more healthy and appetising these days, many cafés confirmed that ownership of an espresso machine doesn't guarantee competency in its use. Stick with major coffee brands like Illy, Atomic, Vittorio or L'Affare and you won't go too wrong.

NORTH ISLAND

North Island Routes

Cape Reinga

Kaitaia

Dargaville

Whangarei

Auckland

Thames

Waihi

Tauranga

Whakatane

Hamilton

Opotiki

Te Kuiti

Rotorua

Taupo

Gisborne

Taumarunui

New Plymouth

Turangi

Wairoa

Hawera

Napier

Wanganui

Bulls

Palmerston North

Woodville

Masterton

Wellington

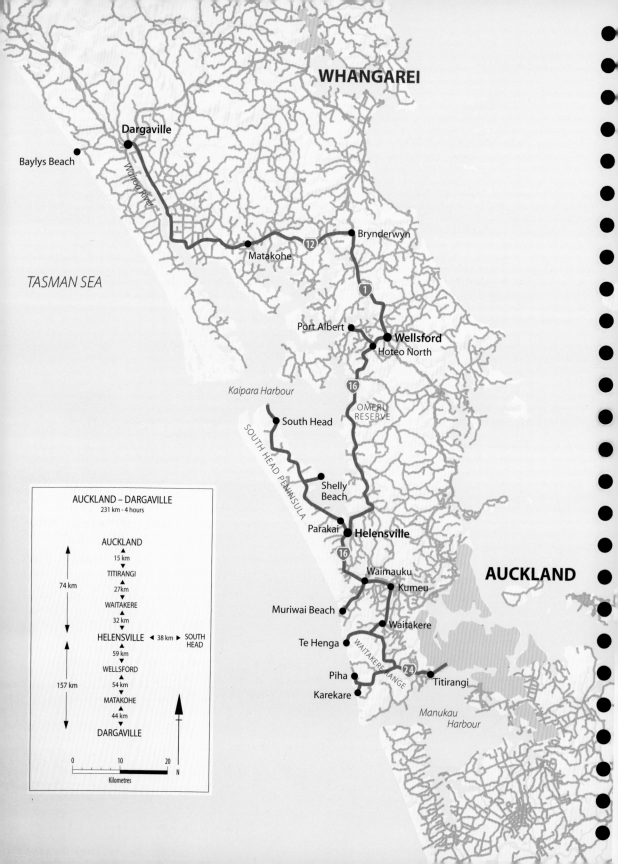

WHANGAREI

Dargaville

Baylys Beach

Wairoa River

TASMAN SEA

Matakohe

Brynderwyn

(12)

(1)

Port Albert

Wellsford

Hoteo North

Kaipara Harbour

(16)

OMERU
RESERVE

South Head

SOUTH HEAD PENINSULA

Shelly
Beach

Parakai

Helensville

(16)

Waimauku

Kumeu

AUCKLAND

Muriwai Beach

Waitakere

Te Henga

WAITAKERE RANGE

(24)

Piha

Titirangi

Karekare

*Manukau
Harbour*

AUCKLAND – DARGAVILLE
231 km - 4 hours

AUCKLAND
▲
15 km
▼
TITIRANGI
▲
27km
▼
WAITAKERE
▲
32 km
▼
HELENSVILLE ◄ 38 km ► SOUTH
HEAD
▲
59 km
▼
WELLSFORD
▲
54 km
▼
MATAKOHE
▲
44 km
▼
DARGAVILLE

74 km

157 km

0   10   20

Kilometres

N

Northland

The motoring tourist in Northland is well catered for by the 'Twin Coast Discovery Highway'. Although the awkward title suggests a single continuous road, the 'highway' is in fact a combination of major and secondary roads (all sealed and in good order) that describes a circular journey around Northland from Auckland. The highway thus links the major west Auckland and Northland attractions: the Waitakere Range, the west coast beaches at Piha, Bethells Beach and Muriwai, Northland's kauri forests, Kaipara and Hokianga harbours, Cape Reinga, Doubtless Bay and the Bay of Islands.

The Discovery Highway is described below in a clockwise direction, and divided into western, Kaitaia–Cape Reinga, and eastern sections. SH 1, the major route north from Auckland, lacks the charm of Discovery Highway, though it is useful as quick access to different sections of it. For notes on SH 1 see the eastern section.

Discovery Highway (Western Section)
Auckland–Dargaville–Hokianga Harbour–Kaitaia

Auckland–Dargaville SH 16, 11, 19, 24
231 km, 4 hours
From central Auckland travel west on SH 16 (motorway) and exit at Waterview/Great North Rd, following SH 11, 19 and then 24 to Titirangi.

Waitakere Range – campgrounds, walks, swimming
The Discovery Highway offers fine views over Auckland as it wends its way on SH 24 through leafy Titirangi and up into the forested Waitakere Range (with luck you'll avoid the Auckland drivers who treat Waitakere Range roads and other motorists with little respect). About 10 km from Titirangi is the Arataki Visitor Centre where you'll find information about the natural history and walks in the ranges. Ten kilometres from the centre is the turnoff to Piha, one of three impressive surf beaches accessed on this section. Karekare Beach (made famous by *The Piano*) is reached from the Piha road, while Te Henga (Bethells Beach) is reached from Waitakere township. SH 24 ends at Kumeu where the Discovery Highway rejoins SH 16.

Kumeu
A little way south of Kumeu on SH 16 are several notable wine producers: Nobilos, Selaks and Coopers Creek, each offering cafés and winetasting. Five kilometres north of Kumeu at Waimauku is the turnoff to Muriwai Beach (10 km) where the highlights are New Zealand's northernmost Australasian gannet colony, fur seals, coastal walks, swimming and surfing.

Waitakere Range

Helensville

The Discovery Highway reaches the southern end of Kaipara Harbour at Helensville where you'll get good food and coffee at the Upper Crust Café. A worthwhile side journey is along the South Head Peninsula (45 minutes to South Head from Helensville on a sealed road) with fine views, swimming at Shelly Beach and Mosquito Bay, sea and freshwater fishing, hot pools at Parakai and the café MacNut Farms Macadamia Farm.

Kaipara Harbour

From Helensville the Discovery Highway (still on SH 16), follows the Kaipara River then turns inland and works around Kaipara Harbour. Several small reserves offer picnic sites and walks along the way. Omeru Reserve (signposted 18 km from Helensville) contains a Maori pa site, and a stand of tall totara and kauri; Port Albert is the site of an historic settlement on the edge of Kaipara Harbour 8 km from SH 16 (turn off 1.6 km north of Hoteo North). It's a pleasant, quiet spot for lunch, with camping and toilet facilities. A highpoint overlooking the harbour is reached before the descent towards Wellsford where the Discovery Highway links briefly with SH 1.

Matakohe

North of Wellsford, turn west at Brynderwyn onto SH 12 and drive 26 km to Matakohe where the famous Matakohe kauri museum is located. Here, in displays, exhibits and photographs, the history is told of how the once vast Northland kauri forests were logged unrelentingly through the nineteenth and early twentieth centuries. Allow at least a couple of hours here then drive away and marvel at how hard the pioneer farmers and road builders had to work to create the landscape before you. You might then reflect on how little of the old forest remains, and be thankful that New Zealand's earliest conservationists succeeded in reserving any of Northland's forest at all.

Dargaville – campground
At Dargaville on the north bank of the wide and muddy Wairoa River the maritime museum is worth a visit and the Blah Blah Blah Café and Uno Restaurant offer good food and coffee. However, the choice eatery in the area is the Funky Fish Café at the magnificent Baylys Beach 15 km west of Dargaville (turn off SH 12, 4 km from the town centre). From Dargaville the Discovery Highway continues up SH 12, but SH 14 offers a quick (1 hour) route to Whangarei for those travelling east.

Tane Mahuta, Waipoua Forest

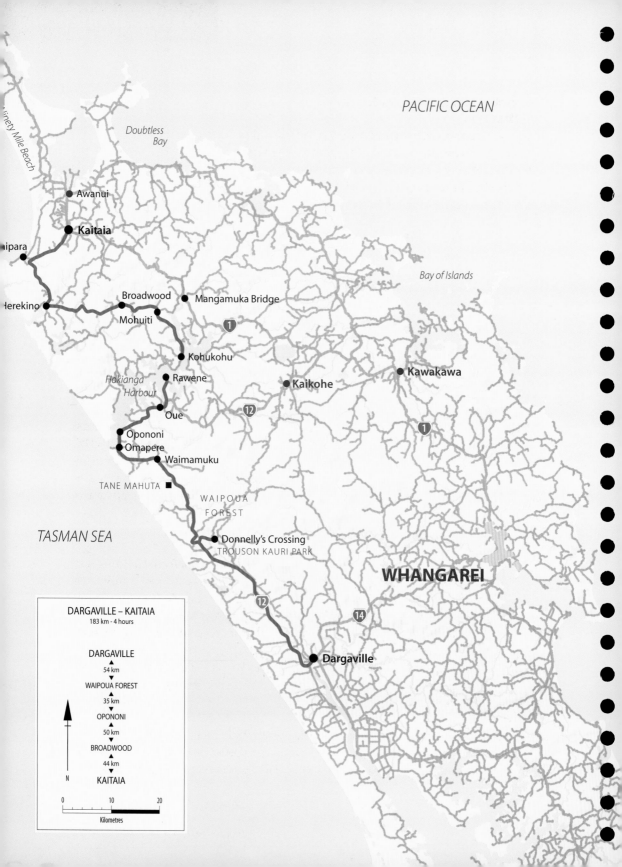

PACIFIC OCEAN

Doubtless Bay

Ninety Mile Beach

● Awanui

● **Kaitaia**

Bay of Islands

ipara ●

Herekino ●

● Broadwood   ● Mangamuka Bridge

Mohuiti

①

● Kawakawa

● Kohukohu

● Rawene   ● **Kaikohe**

Hokianga Harbour

⑫

①

● Oue

● Opononi
● Omapere
● Waimamuku

TANE MAHUTA ■

WAIPOUA FOREST

TASMAN SEA

● Donnelly's Crossing
TROUSON KAURI PARK

WHANGAREI

⑫

⑭

● Dargaville

DARGAVILLE – KAITAIA
183 km - 4 hours

DARGAVILLE
▲
54 km
▼
WAIPOUA FOREST
▲
35 km
▼
OPONONI
▲
50 km
▼
BROADWOOD
▲
44 km
▼
KAITAIA

N

0   10   20

Kilometres

Dargaville–Kaitaia via Hokianga Harbour SH 12
189 km, 4 hours

This leg of the Discovery Highway is equal to anywhere on the South Island's West Coast. By the fastest route (via Kaikohe and SH 1), Dargaville to Kaitaia can be travelled in just over three hours, but there's little point in doing that. Allow a day, drive slowly, enjoy the walks at Trounson's Kauri Park and Waipoua Forest, then catch the vehicle ferry from Rawene across Hokianga Harbour and follow the back roads to Ahipara and Kaitaia.

Trounson Kauri Park – campground, walks, picnicking

Trounson is down a well marked side road off SH 12, 30 km north of Dargaville. (If coming from the north, an unsealed road to the park via Donnelly's Crossing leaves SH 12 about 6 km from the Waipoua Forest Visitor Centre). This large (573 ha) forest remnant contains some superb kauri, viewed from an easy 40-minute loop track suitable for all ages and even those in wheelchairs. Despite the cheesy poetry dressed up as natural history interpretation, one can learn much about kauri and other forest trees and wildlife on this walk. The Department of Conservation manages the area as a 'mainland island' which involves intensive predator and weed control, so what you experience is a very healthy native forest and kiwi habitat compared with other forests in the region.

Waipoua Forest – campground, walks

Flanked by huge kauri, rata, kohekohe and other large trees, the almost 20 km drive through Waipoua Forest is the highlight of the western section of the Discovery Highway. The park was created in 1952, and its natural and social history are described at the visitor centre which arguably offers a more balanced view of Northland's logging and gumdigging past than other places. A lookout 3 km south of the centre offers a fine view, while the easy five minute walk (8 km north of the centre) to Tane Mahuta, the largest known kauri, is a 'must do'.

Hokianga Harbour

Continuing north, petrol can be bought at Waimamaku soon after Waipoua Forest, then Hokianga Harbour appears unexpectedly, beyond a rise with a view across the harbour to an enormous dune on its north bank. The Crystal Café above Omapere is good place to stop and enjoy the vista before continuing on to Opononi. Shortly after Oue, the Discovery Highway turns left off SH 12 and makes for Rawene (Kaikohe is a 45-minute drive on SH 12 for those who want to travel east to SH 1). At Rawene the ferry to Kohukohu ($13) departs on the half-hour (from Kohukohu it leaves on the hour). A walk on Rawene's mangrove forest boardwalk, a bite to eat at the Boathouse Café or a stroll amongst the village's colonial buildings (Clendon House) are pleasant ways to pass time waiting for the ferry.

Kohukohu – Kaitaia (74 km)

From Kohukohu, the Discovery Highway takes you north along the edge of Hokianga Harbour before an enjoyable drive west through farmland and regenerating forest, past Broadwood and Herekino, towards Ahipara at the bottom of Ninety Mile Beach and the turnoff to Kaitaia. Alternately, you may drive east to SH 1 from Mohuiti to Mangamuka Bridge.

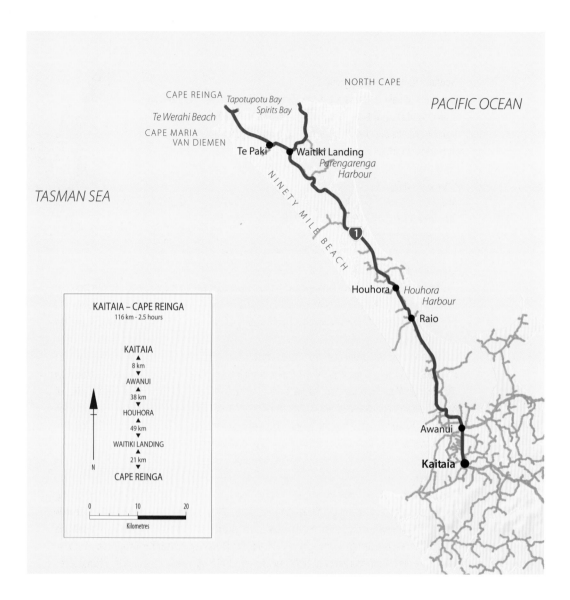

Kaitaia–Cape Reinga SH 1
116 km, 2.5 hours

The Discovery Highway reaches its most northern point at Cape Reinga. The drive takes in pleasant Northland farmland for much of the way, crossing flats north of Kaitaia, and into more undulating grass-covered dunes and pine plantations further north with fine views over Parengarenga Harbour before Waitiki Landing.

 Awanui
The Ancient Kauri Kingdom at Awanui features giant kauri logs, kauri crafts and furniture, and offers good food and coffee at the café.

Houhora Harbour – campground

Just south of Raio is a signposted turnoff to the Waggener Park Museum and campground, sited idyllically on the edge of Houhora Harbour. There's little to tempt taste buds at the café here, though the museum will attract those with an interest in pioneer-era artefacts.

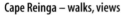

Waitiki Landing

After climbing to a high dune ridge with views of Parengarenga Harbour's inlets and mangrove forests, the road reaches Waitiki Landing where there is a store, petrol and accommodation and information.

Cape Reinga – walks, views

The tarseal ends at Waitiki Landing and the last 21 km to Cape Reinga should be driven with care as it climbs and winds through regenerating scrublands and forests, and distinctive outcrops and cuttings of red volcanic rock. Shortly before the carpark at Cape Reinga is a turnoff to Tapotupotu Bay (picnic site and campground).

Cape Reinga, the lighthouse and views across extensive dunelands and remote clifflines are the main attractions at the road end. A short walk north leads to the lighthouse. The Cape is particularly significant in Maori spiritual belief as the place where the spirits of their dead depart for the place of their ancestors. Eastwards on a fine day is a view toward North Cape while northwards the Tasman Sea and the Pacific Ocean crash together in foamy swells and lines of waves over the Columbia Bank. Below the carpark to the south is Te Werahi Beach and Cape Maria van Diemen.

Cape walks

A turnoff west at Te Paki (about 6 km from Waitiki Landing) down Te Paki Stream Rd leads to stunning dune walks from the road end (picnic site) towards Ninety Mile Beach. Similarly, a 30-minute dune walk from Te Werahi Gate leads to Te Werahi Beach and impressive coastal scenery in the vicinity of Cape Maria van Diemen. At Cape Reinga, walks lead to Te Werahi Beach and Tapotupotu Bay. Information on these walks (and the Te Paki Farm Park which encompasses much of the Cape Reinga area) can be found at the DoC office at Te Paki.

Waitiki Landing–Spirits Bay

From Waitiki Landing a winding unsealed road through a Muriwhenua Incorporation forestry area leads to Spirits Bay where there is a DoC campground and wild beach. The drive offers excellent views of Parengarenga Harbour before the steep descent to Spirits Bay.

NB: Driving Ninety Mile Beach is not recommended for ordinary vehicles. Bus tours are the safest way to experience this stretch of coast.

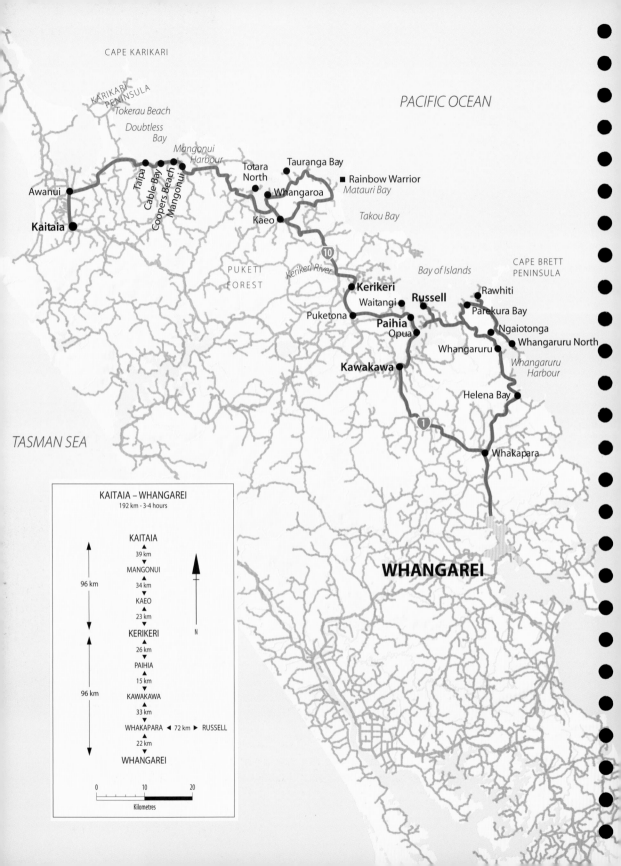

CAPE KARIKARI

KARIKARI PENINSULA

Tokerau Beach

PACIFIC OCEAN

Doubtless Bay

Mangonui Harbour

Totara North

Tauranga Bay

■ Rainbow Warrior

Awanui

Taipa

Cable Bay

Coopers Beach

Mangonui

Whangaroa

Matauri Bay

Kaitaia

Kaeo

Takou Bay

PUKETI FOREST

Kerikeri River

⑩

Bay of Islands

CAPE BRETT PENINSULA

Kerikeri

Rawhiti

Waitangi

Russell

Parekura Bay

Puketona

Paihia

Ngaiotonga

Opua

Whangaruru North

Whangaruru

Whangaruru Harbour

Kawakawa

Helena Bay

①

Whakapara

TASMAN SEA

WHANGAREI

KAITAIA – WHANGAREI
192 km - 3-4 hours

KAITAIA
▲
39 km
▼
MANGONUI
▲
34 km
▼
KAEO
▲
23 km
▼
KERIKERI
▲
26 km
▼
PAIHIA
▲
15 km
▼
KAWAKAWA
▲
33 km
▼
WHAKAPARA ◄ 72 km ► RUSSELL
▲
22 km
▼
WHANGAREI

96 km

96 km

N

0   10   20
Kilometres

Discovery Highway (Eastern Section)
Kaitaia–Whangarei via Doubtless Bay and Bay of Islands SH 10, 11, 1
192 km, 3-4 hours

Northland's sublime east coast beaches and coastal resorts are a direct contrast to the forests, harbours and lesser-developed character of the west. The route described follows the 'Twin Coast Discovery Highway' through Doubtless Bay and the Bay of Islands.

Doubtless Bay – swimming, fishing
From Kaitaia the Discovery Highway sweeps east from Awanui (SH 10) towards the golden beaches of Doubtless Bay. Tokerau Beach on the Karikari Peninsula is reached from an intersection 15 km from Awanui. Then in quick succession, as SH 10 rounds the bay, come the resort villages of Taipa, Cable Bay, Coopers Beach and Mangonui. There's no shortage of good eateries for both wealthy resident and traveller, among them Taipa's Flame Tree Restaurant and Mangonui's Waterfront Café and the Slung Anchor Bar. The wharf in Mangonui remains a popular fishing spot, though locals claim (as they seem to everywhere) 'the fishing isn't as good as it was'. Dolphin-watch tours operate from here.

Whangaroa Harbour – campground, swimming, fishing
Thirty kilometres from Mangonui is the scenic and sheltered Whangaroa Harbour. The harbour is surrounded by steep hills and volcanic plugs including the prominent St Paul on the skyline opposite Whangaroa above Totara North. The harbour is a deep-sea fishing base, and harbour cruises are popular. The 'scenic drive' signposted here is unsealed beyond the turnoff to Tauranga Bay – where there is a great beach and campground.

Kaeo – walking
Kaeo services the surrounding farming and horticultural area. Janit's Texas Diner 2 km north of the town has a good reputation for those in need of steak and country cooking. 16 km west of Kaeo is Puketi Forest which can be accessed from Waiare Rd (turnoff south of Kaeo, unsealed). The Puketi Nature Trail involves a 1 hour loop through kauri/podocarp forest which also protects rare birds such as the kaka and kokako.

Paihia, Bay of Islands

Matauri Bay – campground, fishing
A short distance from Kaeo is the turnoff to Matauri Bay, a settlement populated by Nga Puhi who own and run the popular holiday park there. On the headland overlooking the bay is the striking memorial to the Rainbow Warrior – icon of New Zealand's antinuclear advocacy in the 1980s. The boat, bombed by

French government agents in Auckland in 1986, now rests on the seabed off the Cavalli Islands northeast of here. The short climb to the memorial by sculptor Chris Booth is a pilgrimage everyone should make.

Kerikeri – campground, walks, picnicking

Kerikeri township (turn off SH 10, 23 km from Kaeo) lies on the Kerikeri River in the Bay of Islands. Renowned for its Maori and European settler history, it is also a centre for crafts, culture and kiwifruit. Below the township in Kerikeri Basin is Kemp House, a former mission station built between 1821 and 1822, the oldest standing building in the country. Nearby is the Stone Store, a fine example of nineteenth century stonemasonry completed in 1835, while on the hill behind Kemp House is the weatherboard St James Church, dating from 1878. Remains of the once heavily pallisaded Kororipo Pa can be reached by a short interpreted walk from the Stone Store. Opposite Kemp House next to the information centre is Rewa's village, a re-creation of an unfortified village that stood on the site in the nineteenth century. Kerikeri has numerous eateries and bars but the Rocket Café on Kerikeri Rd north of the town centre stands out for its coffee and good food.

Waitangi/Paihia/Opua

Waitangi and nearby Paihia are 26 km from Kerikeri on SH 11 (turn off SH 10 at Puketona). Waitangi National Reserve is one of the outstanding historic reserves in the country. Here, New Zealand's founding document, the Treaty of Waitangi, was signed by Maori and the British Crown in 1840. Audiovisual presentations and historical displays at the reserve's visitor centre, and the *son et lumière* in the Whare Runanga (meeting house) are highlights of a visit here. Although the presentations skirt contemporary grievances against the treaty, and say little about how Maori were treated after it was signed, they offer nonetheless

Stone Store and St James Church, Kerikeri

a valuable introduction to New Zealand history. There is a café, and opportunity for walks in the Treaty Grounds and to nearby Haruru Falls.

Paihia has several good cafés (try Poco Loco Café on the waterfront) and places to swim or picnic. At the busy waterfront information centre you can organise bay cruises, fishing, dolphin and whale-watching. The vehicle ferry departs Opua, 5 km south of Paihia, every 10 minutes between 6.50 a.m. and 10 p.m. in summer and until 8.45 p.m. in winter.

The coastal forest walk through Harrison Scenic Reserve (30 mins) at Opua is highly recommended. Allow an hour (67 km) to reach Whangarei from Opua via Kawakawa and SH 1.

Russell – campground, walks, swimming, fishing

As well as occupying a significant place in New Zealand's early European history, Russell is a major holiday spot and headquarters of the Bay of Islands' Maritime and Historical Park. A number of historic buildings and the Russell Museum are of note here.

Russell–SH 1 at Whakapara via Whangaruru Harbour (1 hour)

You can of course return by ferry to Opua, but a highly recommended alternative is to make this scenic drive which takes in the eastern Bay of Islands' bays, inlets, forests and Whangaruru Harbour. Remote beaches and camping sites are a feature of the drive. From Russell the route (sealed) passes Parekura Bay at the base of Cape Brett Peninsula then turns southeast towards Ngaiotonga and Whangaruru Harbour. From Helena Bay the route heads south to Whakapara. Unsealed roads lead from this route to Rawhiti and the beginning of the Cape Brett Track, and to Whangaruru North Head where there is a popular campsite and 45-minute (one way) walk to the head for outstanding views.

Motuarohia Island, Bay of Islands

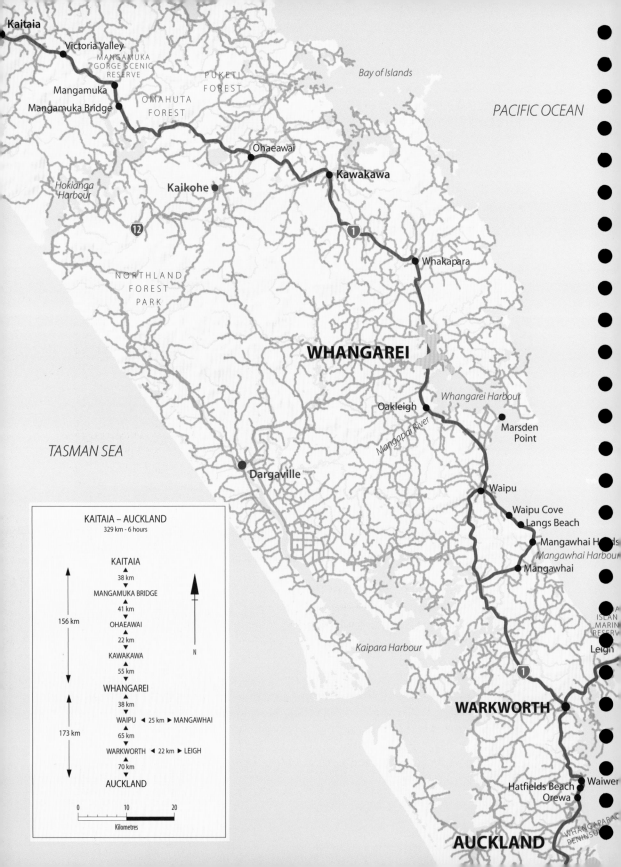

Kaitaia

Victoria Valley

MANGAMUKA
GORGE SCENIC
RESERVE

Mangamuka

Mangamuka Bridge

OMAHUTA
FOREST

PUKETI
FOREST

Bay of Islands

PACIFIC OCEAN

Ohaeawai

Kawakawa

Hokianga
Harbour

Kaikohe

12

NORTHLAND
FOREST
PARK

Whakapara

WHANGAREI

Whangarei Harbour

Oakleigh

Marsden
Point

TASMAN SEA

Mangapai River

Dargaville

Waipu

Kaipara Harbour

Waipu Cove
Langs Beach
Mangawhai Heads
Mangawhai Harbour
Mangawhai

ISLAN
MARIN
RESERV

Leigh

WARKWORTH

Hatfields Beach
Orewa

Waiwer

WHANGAPARA
PENINSU

AUCKLAND

KAITAIA – AUCKLAND
329 km - 6 hours

KAITAIA
▲ 38 km
MANGAMUKA BRIDGE
▲ 41 km
OHAEAWAI
▲ 22 km
KAWAKAWA
▲ 55 km
WHANGAREI
▲ 38 km
WAIPU ◄ 25 km ► MANGAWHAI
▲ 65 km
WARKWORTH ◄ 22 km ► LEIGH
▲ 70 km
AUCKLAND

156 km

173 km

N

0   10   20
Kilometres

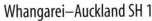

Kaitaia–Whangarei SH 1
156 km, 3 hours

This is the quick route from Kaitaia to Whangarei, Hokianga Harbour and Bay of Islands, however the road is often busier, and generally lacks the charms of the east and west coast drives. Petrol and other services are available at most centres. Its scenic highlights are the crossing of the Mangamuka Gorge Scenic Reserve, which begins 16 km from Kaitaia at Victoria Valley, and views across Puketi and Omahuta Forests after Mangamuka Bridge. A turnoff at Mangamuka Bridge provides quick access to the northern Hokianga Harbour. At Ohaeawai is the turnoff to SH 12 to Kaikohe (12 km), the kauri forests and Dargaville.

Whangarei–Auckland SH 1
173 km, 3 hours

South of the city, SH 1 rounds Whangarei Harbour and just after Oakleigh crosses the estuary formed by the Mangapai River. The turnoff to Marsden Point is 15 km past Oakleigh, for those interested in visiting New Zealand's sole oil refinery.

Waipu environs – campground, walks, swimming, fishing
Seekers of beaches and coastal scenery should leave SH 1 at Waipu (38 km from Whangarei) and follow the Discovery Highway to Waipu Cove, Langs Beach, Mangawhai Heads and Mangawhai. The beaches are excellent and tourists and holidaymakers are well catered for. The Mangawhai Cliffs Walkway from Mangawhai Heads is a recommended walk in this area.

Warkworth
Boutique wineries, cafés, an art and craft trail, and numerous attractive beaches are features of the Warkworth area. A trip to Leigh and to the Goat Island Marine Reserve (24 km) is one of the highlights – snorkelling and diving in the 'no fishing' reserve is often rewarded with remarkable encounters with large snapper and moki. The Sawmill Café, just out of Leigh towards the reserve, is an excellent establishment.

Hauraki Gulf

Twenty-three km south of Warkworth are the popular Waiwera thermal springs. Seaside resorts at Hatfields Beach and Orewa soon follow, and those in exploratory mood and/or not yet bored by sublime coastlines should drive out to Whangaparaoa Peninsula. Shakespear Regional Park on its eastern extremity is open to the public for walks and camping. The final leg of the Discovery Highway is along the motorways to central and western Auckland that cut inland south of Orewa.

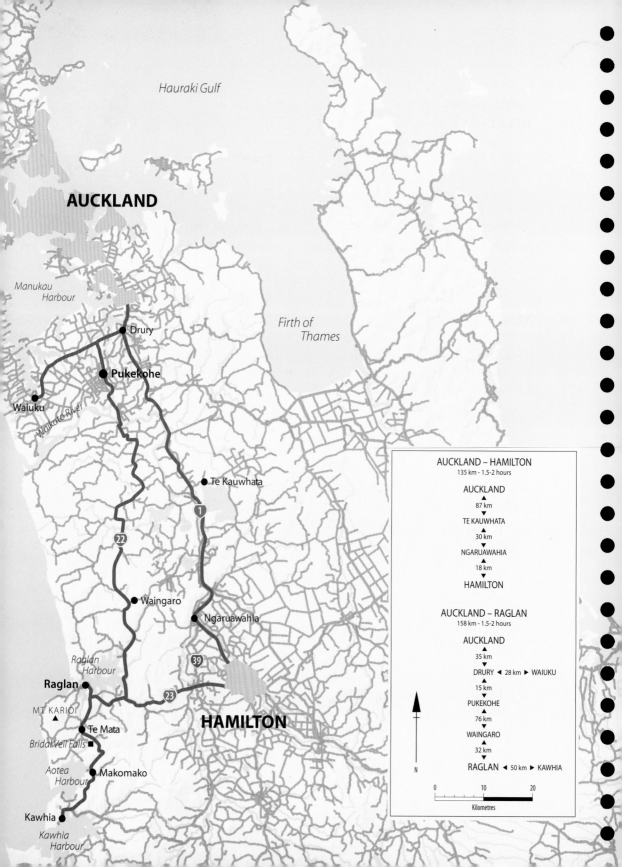

Hauraki Gulf

AUCKLAND

Manukau
Harbour

Firth of
Thames

Waikato River

● Drury

● **Pukekohe**

● Waiuku

● Te Kauwhata

①

㉒

● Waingaro

● Ngaruawahia

㊱

Raglan
Harbour

㉓

Raglan ●

MT KARIOI ▲

● Te Mata

Bridal Veil Falls ■

Aotea
Harbour

● Makomako

HAMILTON

Kawhia ●

Kawhia
Harbour

AUCKLAND – HAMILTON
135 km - 1.5-2 hours

AUCKLAND
▲
87 km
▼
TE KAUWHATA
▲
30 km
▼
NGARUAWAHIA
▲
18 km
▼
HAMILTON

AUCKLAND – RAGLAN
158 km - 1.5-2 hours

AUCKLAND
▲
35 km
▼
DRURY ◄ 28 km ► **WAIUKU**
▲
15 km
▼
PUKEKOHE
▲
76 km
▼
WAINGARO
▲
32 km
▼
RAGLAN ◄ 50 km ► **KAWHIA**

N

0   10   20
Kilometres

Auckland–Hamilton SH 1
135 km, 1.5–2 hours

The drive to Hamilton down SH 1 involves one of the busiest stretches of motorway and highway in New Zealand. Consequently, there's no shortage of places to refuel or find a meal at any of the centres en route. Wineries at Te Kauwhata (87 km from Auckland) include the Rongopai winery which has a pleasant café. One kilometre south of Ngaruawahia is the equally pleasant Country Café. The SH 39 turnoff to Otorohanga (68 km to Otorohanga) is useful to note as it offers a bypass around Hamilton and access to Raglan and Kawhia harbours.

Auckland–Waiuku–Raglan via Pukekohe SH 22
158 km, 1.5–2 hours

This route to Raglan is more scenic and the roads are quieter than travel via SH 1 and Hamilton. To reach Pukekohe, leave the Auckland motorway at Drury and turn onto SH 22. The route then follows SH 22 until it meets SH 23, 14 km east of Raglan.

Waiuku/Awhitu Peninsula – campground, swimming, picnicking
Waiuku (28 km from Drury, 50 minutes from central Auckland), a charming rural town at the base of the Awhitu Peninsula on the edge of Manukau Harbour, is worth visiting for its historic buildings, pioneer museum and beaches and campgrounds on the peninsula.

Pukekohe–Raglan
108 km, 1.5 hours
Pukekohe (50 km from Auckland) is a bustling town servicing the surrounding market gardening region. The drive to Raglan winds through undulating plains and hill country and occasional forest remnants including a fine stand of totara at St Albans near Waingaro. Hot springs at Waingaro have been developed into an attractive spa – a fun place for families, with an adjacent motorcamp and tavern. The last few kilometres to the SH 23 junction are unsealed.

Raglan – campground, swimming, picnicking, fishing
A justly popular holiday resort on the edge of Raglan Harbour. Renowned for its surf beaches, the settlement has a laid back holiday feel. There are several cafés: Tongue in Groove on the main street appears to be the place to hang out, though, like the Marlin Café at the wharf, they charge Auckland prices for a coffee. Walks to Mt Karioi from the coast and the Bridal Veil Falls near Te Mata are popular. The 50 km 'back route' to Kawhia along Raglan Rd via Te Mata and Makomako is a recommended scenic drive though it is two-thirds unsealed and requires care. Allow an hour from Raglan to reach Hamilton along SH 23.

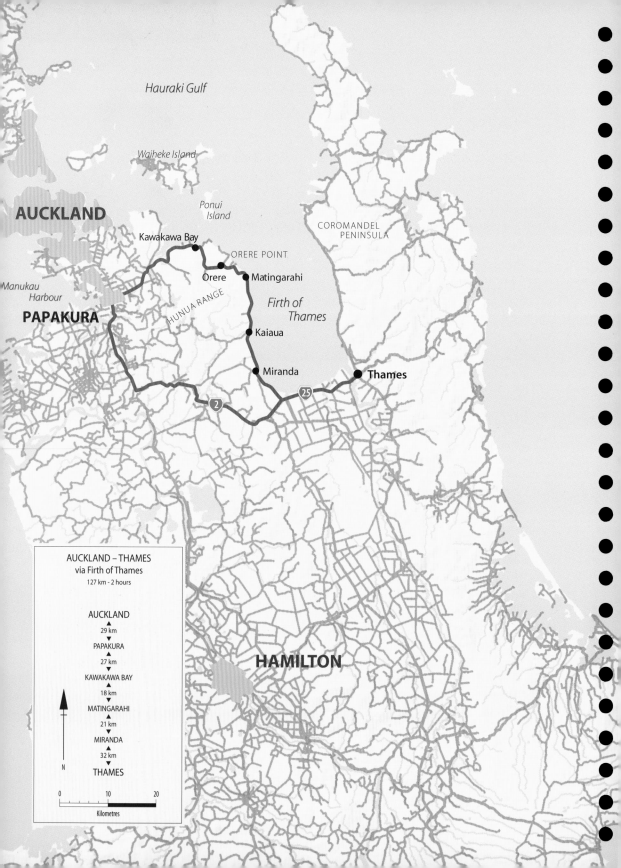

Hauraki Gulf

Waiheke Island

AUCKLAND

Ponui Island

COROMANDEL PENINSULA

Manukau Harbour

Kawakawa Bay

ORERE POINT

PAPAKURA

Orere

Matingarahi

HUNUA RANGE

Firth of Thames

Kaiaua

Miranda

Thames

25

2

HAMILTON

AUCKLAND – THAMES
via Firth of Thames
127 km - 2 hours

AUCKLAND
▲
29 km
▼
PAPAKURA
▲
27 km
▼
KAWAKAWA BAY
▲
18 km
▼
MATINGARAHI
▲
21 km
▼
MIRANDA
▲
32 km
▼
THAMES

N

0   10   20
Kilometres

Auckland–Thames SH 2, 25
127 km, 2 hours

The quickest route from Auckland to Thames is via SHs 2 and 25 and takes 90 minutes, however, I'd recommend the scenic drive from Papakura that skirts the Firth of Thames and the base of the Hunua Range. At Kawakawa Bay views spread north to Waiheke and Ponui Islands, then a climb through forested Te Morehu Scenic Reserve leads to Orere and the Orere Point campground. The road narrows between Matingarahi and Kaiaua (apparently the best fish and chips in New Zealand here). At Miranda is the Miranda Shorebird Centre, the first point of call for exploring the internationally important wading bird reserve in the firth just over the road. Miranda's other attraction is its hot springs. From Miranda it's about 32 km to Thames.

West coast, Coromandel Peninsula

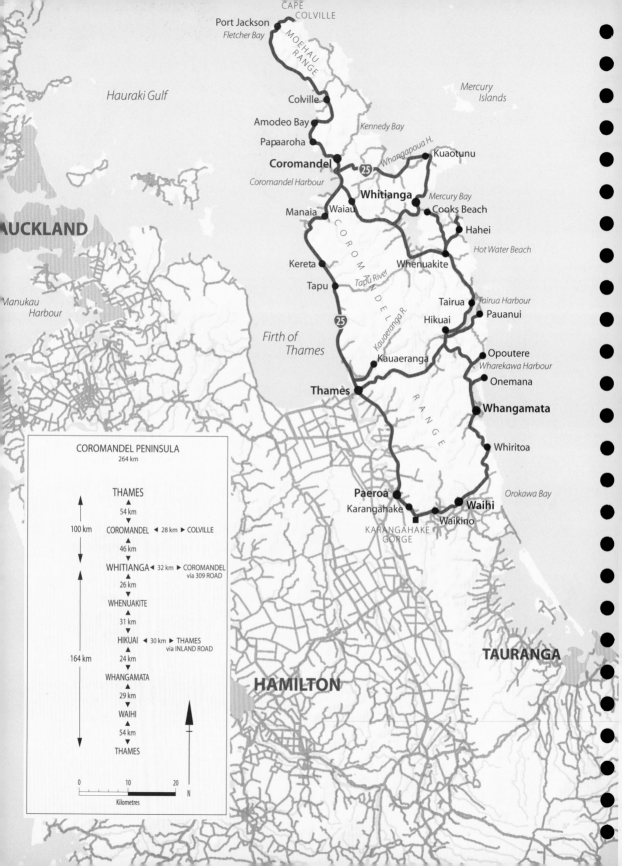

CAPE COLVILLE

Port Jackson
Fletcher Bay

MOEHAU RANGE

Hauraki Gulf

Colville

Amodeo Bay

Papaaroha

Kennedy Bay

Mercury Islands

Coromandel

Kuaotunu

Coromandel Harbour

Whangapoua H.

25

Whitianga

Mercury Bay

Cooks Beach

Manaia

Waiau

Hahei

Kereta

Whenuakite

Hot Water Beach

Tapu River

Tapu

COROMANDEL

AUCKLAND

Kauaeranga R.

Tairua

Tairua Harbour

Hikuai

Pauanui

25

Firth of Thames

Manukau Harbour

Kauaeranga

Opoutere

Wharekawa Harbour

Onemana

Thames

RANGE

Whangamata

Whiritoa

Paeroa

Orokawa Bay

Karangahake

Waihi

Waikino

KARANGAHAKE GORGE

TAURANGA

HAMILTON

COROMANDEL PENINSULA
264 km

THAMES
▲
54 km
▼
COROMANDEL ◄ 28 km ► COLVILLE
▲
46 km
▼
WHITIANGA ◄ 32 km ► COROMANDEL
via 309 ROAD
▲
26 km
▼
WHENUAKITE
▲
31 km
▼
HIKUAI ◄ 30 km ► THAMES
via INLAND ROAD
▲
24 km
▼
WHANGAMATA
▲
29 km
▼
WAIHI
▲
54 km
▼
THAMES

100 km

164 km

0   10   20
Kilometres

N

Coromandel Peninsula SH 25, 25a
Circuit 264 km

Coromandel is one of the North Island's top holiday destinations so expect the place to be crowded through January and February. Sheltered bays and harbours, the Coromandel Range, a thriving arts, crafts and alternative lifestyles community, and a long Maori and European history are among the attractions.

Thames–Coromandel SH 25
54 km, 1 hour

Thames – campground, walks
Thames' attractions includes its museum (which recounts gold rush and logging eras), and the mineral displays at the mining school. Those interested in arts and crafts can purchase a guide to Coromandel galleries at the Thames Information Centre. East of Thames in the Kauaeranga Valley (14 km) is a DoC visitor centre, a base for camping, walks and information about recreational activities in the Coromandel Range. The working kauri dam is a highlight.

Coromandel
Lined with pohutukawa, the road to Coromandel is a lovely, if sometimes narrow, drive up the western side of the peninsula past bays, beaches, small settlements and craft galleries. At Tapu (19 km), a visit to the Rapaura Watergardens (6.5 km down the Tapu Coroglen Rd) is highly recommended. From Kereta, the road climbs to points overlooking Manaia and Coromandel harbours and the Hauraki Gulf. As you round the mangrove-fringed harbours towards Coromandel look out for stalls selling fresh mussels and oysters.

Coromandel's charm lies in the atmosphere conjured by its sidewalk cafés, galleries and historic buildings dating from the gold rushes of the 1850s and 60s. The mining school has working models of quartz crushing machinery and other nineteenth century mining relics. Gold was struck for the first time in New Zealand at Driving Creek, a few kilometres north of Coromandel. These days Driving Creek is a haven for artisans and location of the famous narrow-gauge Driving Creek railway. Driving Creek also features potteries, working steam engines and a brickworks and a café. Ten minutes past Driving Creek up Kennedy Bay Rd (steep and unsealed) is the Tokatea Lookout and walk – a superb viewpoint.

Colville
Thirty minutes (28 km) north of Coromandel is this friendly village that began Coromandel's reputation for alternative lifestyles. The Colville Caff makes an excellent coffee. Before Colville there are serviced campgrounds at Shelly, Long and Amodeo Bays and at Papaaroha. Legstretcher: The 40-minute coastal forest walk at Papaaroha.

Cape Colville – campground, walks

Many make the scenic drive (unsealed) north around the Moehau Range to Cape Colville/Port Jackson (29 km, 1 hour). However the road is rough. There are DoC campgrounds at Fantail Bay (18 km from Colville) and at Fletcher Bay, five minutes from Port Jackson.

Coromandel–Whitianga SH 25
46 km, 1 hour

Allow 1 hour for the pleasant drive along SH 25 which crosses the Coromandel Range to Whangapoua Harbour and Kuaotunu settlement (petrol, dairy, pleasant beaches and a campground nearby). Then it's a 16 km drive through another fragment of Coromandel Forest Park to Mercury Bay and Whitianga.

Coromandel–Whitianga via the '309 Road'
32 km, 50 minutes

An unsealed scenic route across the Coromandel Range, which begins off SH 25 about 4 km south of Coromandel. Highly recommended by the locals, this is nonetheless a rather narrow and winding drive. Apart from forest scenery, the highlights are the Waiau Waterworks (an eccentric public garden) 9 km from Coromandel, Waiau Falls (popular swimming hole) and the nearby Kauri Grove (12 km, one of the few remaining unlogged kauri stands in the region, allow 30 minutes to walk through here on an easy path).

Whitianga–Waihi
75km, 2 hours

Whitianga – campground, swimming, fishing

Once a major colonial port supporting the trade in kauri and kauri gum, Whitianga is now a rural service town and holiday resort. In summer tourists and holidaymakers gather to enjoy the area's beaches, water activities and coastal scenery. Of the cafés, Nina's is recommended for a good coffee.

Hahei & Cooks Beach – campground, walks, swimming

Two of the Whitianga area's most popular locations. Hahei is 37 km from Whitianga (turnoff at Whenuakite) and its attractions are its beach, the Te Whanganui-A-Hei Marine Reserve and the Cathedral Cove walkway – an excellent interpreted coastal walk (2 hours return) with spectacular scenery. Luna Café in the village makes great coffee. At Hot Water Beach, south of Hahei you can dig out your own natural spa on the beach two hours either side of high tide.

To reach Cooks Beach turn left on Purangi Rd 2 km from the Whenuakite intersection. Cooks is another sublime safe swimming beach, and where Captain Cook and his astronomer observed the transit of Mercury across the sun in 1769. The Shakespeare Cliff walk offers panoramic views of Mercury Bay. It's a short drive from here to Flaxmill Bay and Ferry Landing opposite Whitianga.

Tairua/Pauanui – campground, walk, swimming

Tairua (37 km from Whitianga) is an idyllic settlement near the mouth of Tairua Harbour. Across the harbour (29 km by road), is the exclusive, purpose-built holiday-town of Pauanui, where lawns are perfectly clipped, the streets have pretentious names like Motu Capri, and the wealthy park their ostentatious launches by canal-side homes. The wealth stopped flowing at the shopping centre which resembles that of a South Island hydro-town, nonetheless there is a good surf beach and a rewarding though steep climb up Pauanui Mountain from the south end of Pauanui beach.

At Hikuai, 11 km from Tairua, you can return to Thames (30 km) via SH 25a, which wriggles through the Coromandel Range with excellent views of the Pinnacles along the way. Between Hikuai and Whangamata side roads lead to Opoutere and Onemana beaches. Opoutere is halfway round mangrove-lined Wharekawa Harbour which has a great youth hostel and campground on its shores. Walks in dunelands and to the wildlife reserve (birdwatching) in the harbour estuary are recommended here. Onemana, more developed, has a lovely beach, views to the Alderman Islands, and Palmers Café.

Whangamata – campground, swimming
Whangamata's 3.8 km Ocean Beach has a renowned surf break. Like Whitianga, the population swells in summer and cafés and restaurants have emerged to meet the demand for good food and beverages. Try Vibes Café for a strong coffee with breakfast.

Waihi – campground, walks, swimming
After Whiritoa Beach, SH 25 climbs a hill and descends to Waihi, a modern goldmining town and holiday destination (29 km from Whangamata). Waihi trades on its long mining history with historic walks, relics, museum and vintage railway. If you've never visited an opencast mine, this is the place. Waihi's 'heart of gold', the Martha Mine in the centre of the town, is open for tours, otherwise find the Moresby Ave lookout where interpretation panels would have you believe that ripping open a 300 m deep hole is a most natural and environmentally sensitive activity.

Waihi–Thames via Paeroa
54 km, 1 hour
The highlights of this drive are the Waikino historic mining ruins and the scenic drive through Karangahake Gorge. Among Waikino's attractions are what's left of the largest quartz crushing battery in Australasia. There's a DoC visitor centre, museum, railway and tram rides here too. The Karangahake Gorge Historic Walkway takes in many of the ruins in this area. Waikino is also the centre of an established arts and crafts community. The gorge has picnic sites and safe swimming in the Ohinemuri River.

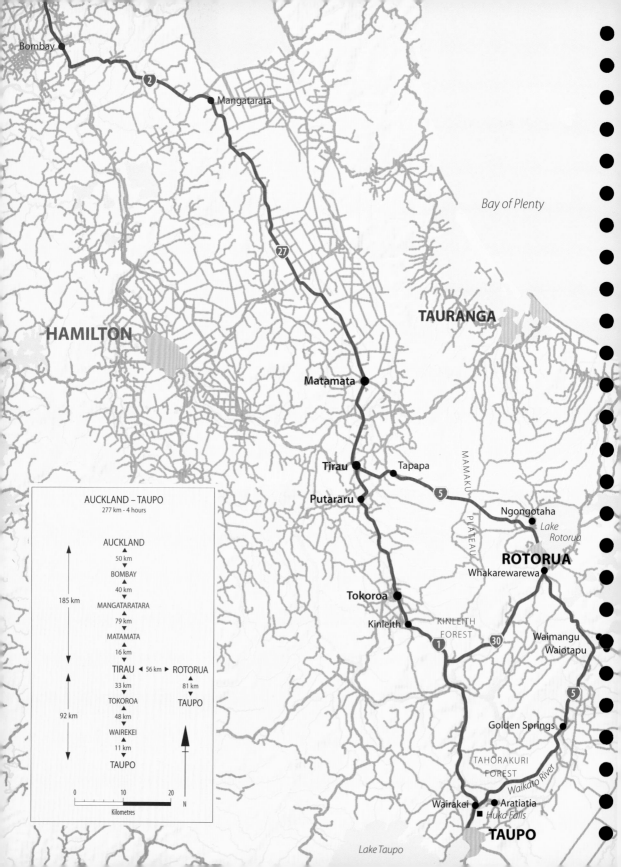

Bombay

② Mangatarata

Bay of Plenty

㉗

TAURANGA

HAMILTON

Matamata

MAMAKU

Tirau   Tapapa

Putaruru   ⑤

PLATEAU   Ngongotaha   *Lake Rotorua*

ROTORUA

Whakarewarewa

Tokoroa   KINLEITH FOREST   ㉚   Waimangu
                                                        Waiotapu
Kinleith   ①

                                        ⑤

                                Golden Springs

TAHORAKURI FOREST   *Waikato River*

Wairakei   ● Aratiatia
                ■ *Huka Falls*

TAUPO

Lake Taupo

AUCKLAND – TAUPO
277 km - 4 hours

AUCKLAND
▲
50 km
▼
BOMBAY
▲
40 km
▼   185 km
MANGATARATARA
▲
79 km
▼
MATAMATA
▲
16 km
▼
TIRAU ◄ 56 km ► ROTORUA
▲   ▲
33 km   81 km
▼   ▼
TOKOROA   TAUPO
▲   92 km
48 km
▼
WAIREKEI
▲
11 km
▼
TAUPO

0   10   20
Kilometres   N

Auckland–Rotorua SH 2, 27, 5

241 km, 3.5 hours

The quickest route from Auckland to Rotorua is via state highways 2 and 27, bypassing Hamilton. Turn onto SH 2 from Auckland's southern motorway (SH 1) south of Bombay, and follow it as far as Mangatarata where it intersects SH 27. Apart from a short hilly section south of here, the road as far as Tirau runs straight through the flat pasturelands of the Piako-Waihou Basin.

Matamata

At Matamata (169 km from Auckland) look out for Workmans Café (the one with the Lambretta scooter permanently parked outside). Three kilometres north of the town on Tower Rd is the Firth Tower Historical Museum featuring the interesting pioneer and Maori history of this area.

Just south of Tirau turn east onto SH 5 to Rotorua. From Tapapa SH 5 climbs onto the forested Mamaku Plateau – lovely driving to Ngongotaha on the shores of Lake Rotorua, 7 km from the Rotorua city centre.

Auckland–Taupo SH 2, 27, 1

277 km, 4 hours

Follow the route above to Tirau where SH 27 rejoins SH 1. From Tirau it's a straight run down SH 1 through Putaruru, the mill towns of Tokoroa and Kinleith and long avenues of pine plantations in Kinleith Forest. This is a very busy road with articulated freight trucks, log haulers and idiots in fast cars all trying to outdo each other. (Allow 40 minutes to reach Rotorua via SH 30 which intersects 19 km from Tokoroa.)

Wairakei (campground, sightseeing)/Huka Falls

The Wairakei environs has almost every type of geothermal activity, some of which has been harnessed to produce electricity. A short drive along SH 5 leads to the Aratiatia Rapids on the Waikato River below the Aratiatia dam. Five kilometres south of Wairakei is the turnoff to the spectacular Huka Falls, which is reached after a short easy walk.

Taupo – campground, water activities, walks

Idyllically situated, Taupo is world-renowned as the base for trout fishing on the lake and its tributary rivers. Cafés and bars abound, along with opportunities for fine dining, swimming, adventure sports and more sedate activities like a walk through the gardens of the Waipahihi Botanical Reserve. Lake Taupo's waters fill the crater formed by what's believed to be one of the world's largest volcanic eruptions.

Rotorua–Taupo SH 5

81 km, 1.5 hours

This route skirts the western edge of Kaingaroa Forest and takes in the major geothermal attractions at Whakarewarewa (3 km from Rotorua), Waimangu (25 km) and Waiotapu (30 km). Golden Springs (43 km) has a motorcamp and thermal baths. Beyond here much of the drive to Wairakei travels between the broad forested avenues formed by the Tahorakuri exotic forest. From Wairakei it's 11 km to Taupo. (See above).

HAMILTON

Raglan

▲ MT KARIOI

MT PIRONGIA ▲

Pirongia

Te Awamutu

Whatawhata

Oparau

Kawhia

Kawhia
Harbour

Te Anga

MANGAPOHUE
ARCH

Otorohanga

Waitomo
Caves

Marokopa

Marokopa
Falls

Te Kuiti

Tasman Sea

Piopio

Awakino River

Awakino

Mokau

Tongaporutu

▲ MT MESSENGER

Waitara

Onaero

Urenui

NEW PLYMOUTH

Waitara River

HAMILTON – NEW PLYMOUTH
225 km - 4.5 hours

79 km

146 km

HAMILTON ◄ 94 km ► KAWHIA
via SH 31
▲
30 km
▼
TE AWAMUTU
▲
29 km
▼
OTOROHANGA ◄ 92 km ► KAWHIA
via WAITOMO
▲
20 km
▼
TE KUITI
▲
56 km
▼
AWAKINO
▲
59 km
▼
URENUI
▲
31 km
▼
NEW PLYMOUTH

N

0   10   20

Kilometres

Hamilton–Kawhia SH 23, 31

94 km, 1 hour

The most straightforward way to Kawhia Harbour is to take SH 23 and turn south at Whatawhata towards Pirongia. A good road past Pirongia leads to the SH 31 junction (from Otorohanga). Near Kawhia at Oparau, Bill Rogers at the store is a useful source of local tourist information.

Kawhia – campground, swimming, fishing

Kawhia is not as flashy as Raglan but is no less charming and possesses a strong sense of its Maori and European history. The drive to Ocean Beach offers views across the harbour and towards Mts Pirongia and Karioi, but the highlight are the hot pools that can be dug out on the beach at low tide.

Hamilton–New Plymouth SH 3

225 km, 4.5 hours

I recommend locating (at visitor centres) the free *The Best of the West* heritage trail brochure, one of the better ones of its type, for its useful guide to this region.

Otorohanga

South of Hamilton SH 3 traverses dairying and sheep farming country in the Waipa Basin to Te Awamutu, then continues to Otorohanga. North Island brown kiwi and other native species can be viewed at Otorohanga's Kiwi House.

Waitomo environs – campground, walks

Eight kilometres south of Otorohanga is the turnoff to Waitomo Caves. Tours of these famous limestone caves are arranged from the 'adventure centre' 8 km from the highway. Highly recommended is the drive past Waitomo to Marokopa (1 hour, sealed) on the west coast. On the way are excellent short walks to Marokopa Falls and the magnificent Mangapohue limestone arch. There is a campground and store at Marokopa. Another justifiably popular drive is the back route to Kawhia (1.5 hours, sealed, turn off at Te Anga), which offers fine views and forests as it rounds Kawhia Harbour.

Mokau – campground, swimming, fishing

From the township of Te Kuiti, 20 km from Waitomo, SH 3 turns southwest. After Piopio the road winds through the Awakino Gorge to reach the coast at Awakino and shortly afterwards, the popular resort of Mokau. Twenty minutes south of Mokau at Tongaporutu is the turnoff to the White Cliffs Walkway, an exhilarating walk along limestone seacliffs overlooking the Tasman.

Urenui – campground, swimming, fishing

Between Tongaporutu and Urenui the highway climbs forested Mt Messenger. Back on coastal plains, Urenui is a popular holiday spot, locality for craft artists and the White Cliffs Brewery. A few kilometres south of Urenui at Onaero, a signpost marks the turnoff to Waiau Estate Winery and Café – the best eatery between Hamilton and New Plymouth. There's a campground at Onaero Beach.

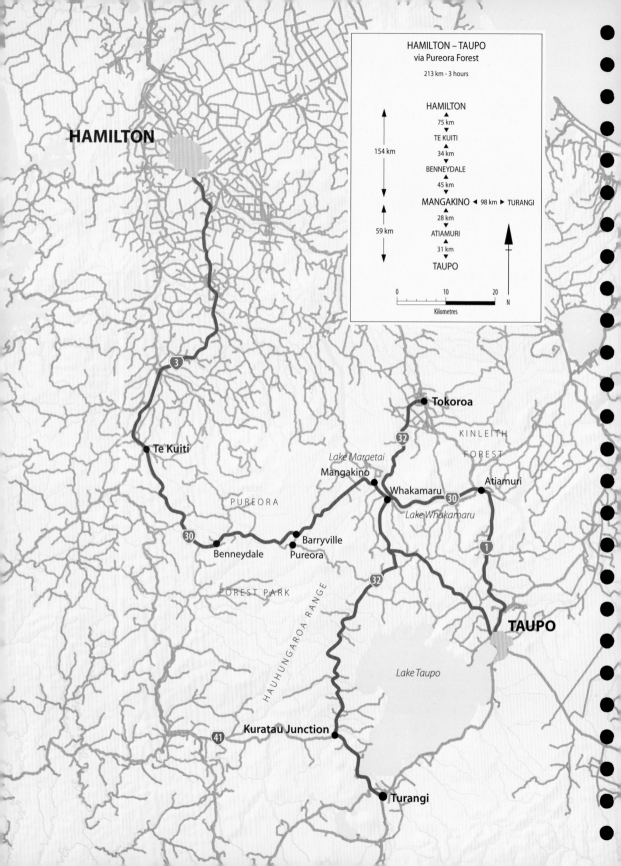

HAMILTON

HAMILTON – TAUPO
via Pureora Forest

213 km - 3 hours

HAMILTON
▲
75 km
▼
TE KUITI
▲
34 km
▼
BENNEYDALE
▲
45 km
▼
MANGAKINO ◄ 98 km ► TURANGI
▲
28 km
▼
ATIAMURI
▲
31 km
▼
TAUPO

154 km

59 km

0   10   20
Kilometres
N

Tokoroa

KINLEITH

FOREST

Te Kuiti

Lake Maraetai
Mangakino
Whakamaru
Atiamuri

PUREORA

Lake Whakamaru

Benneydale
Barryville
Pureora

FOREST PARK

HAUHUNGAROA RANGE

Lake Taupo

TAUPO

Kuratau Junction

Turangi

Hamilton–Taupo via Pureora Forest SH 3, 30, 1
213 km, 3 hours

The highlight of this drive is the 78,000 ha Pureora Forest Park, a remnant of a vast podocarp forest that dominated the area before it was logged.

Drive to Te Kuiti via SH 3 (1.25 hours, see Hamilton–New Plymouth, Route 15). From Te Kuiti, turn onto SH 30 which enters the hilly sheep-farming country west of Benneydale village (store, hotel, petrol). East of Benneydale the road passes briefly through the small forested Herekawa Scenic Reserve then reaches Maraeroa Rd to Pureora after 20 minutes.

Pureora – campground, walks

Follow the gravel road to the Pureora visitor centre, located, ironically perhaps, in a fragment of native forest inside a plantation forest. The ultimately successful battle to save what was left of the tall trees of Pureora was one of the defining moments in New Zealand's conservation history. Two short walks I would recommend are the Totara Walk and the excellent Forest Tower Walk. Totara Walk (close to the centre) is an easy 30-minute loop amongst the enormous trees the area is known for. A self-guide brochure for tree identification is available. The Forest Tower Walk is signposted from Barryville Rd (which returns to SH 30 east of Maraeroa Rd). A short walk leads to the 12 m multilevel forest tower which allows you to climb into the forest canopy. Interpretation panels in the tower identify birds and trees.

Mangakino – campground

A settlement with friendly locals on the banks of Lake Maraetai and on the edge of Kinleith Forest. To reach Taupo, continue along SH 30 beside the Waikato River to the SH 1 junction before Atiamuri.

At Whakamaru SH 30 meets SH 32 which links Tokoroa and Turangi between the western shores of Lake Taupo and the eastern flanks of the Pureora Forest. From this junction allow half an hour to Tokoroa or 1 hour to the junction with SH 41 at Kuratau and a further half-hour to Turangi. A more direct route between Whakamaru and Taupo is to drive south on SH 32 approximately 15 km and take the signposted route east to Taupo.

Pureora Forest

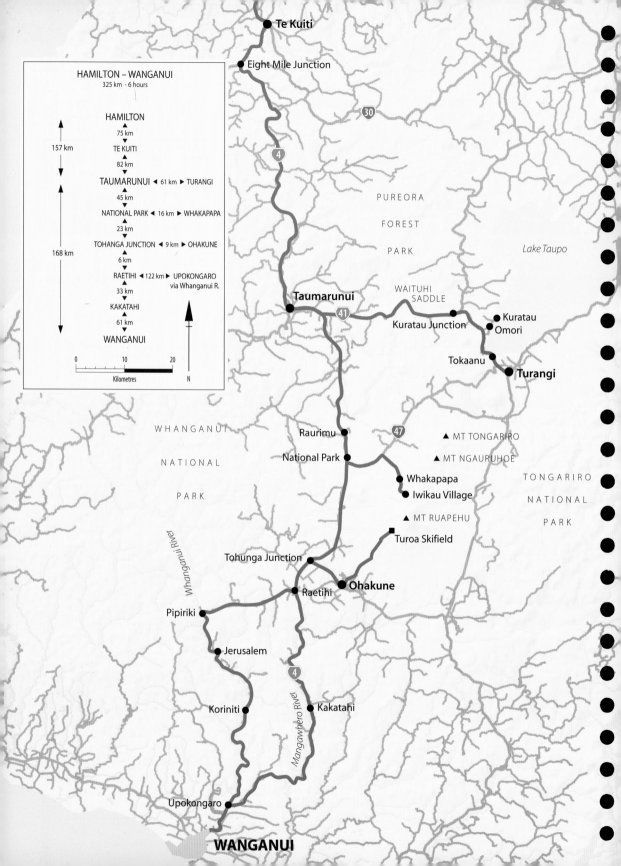

HAMILTON – WANGANUI
325 km - 6 hours

HAMILTON
↓ 75 km
TE KUITI
↓ 82 km
TAUMARUNUI ◄ 61 km ► TURANGI
↓ 45 km
NATIONAL PARK ◄ 16 km ► WHAKAPAPA
↓ 23 km
TOHANGA JUNCTION ◄ 9 km ► OHAKUNE
↓ 6 km
RAETIHI ◄ 122 km ► UPOKONGARO
via Whanganui R.
↓ 33 km
KAKATAHI
↓ 61 km
WANGANUI

157 km

168 km

0   10   20
Kilometres

N

Te Kuiti
Eight Mile Junction
30
4
PUREORA
FOREST
PARK
Lake Taupo
WAITUHI
SADDLE
Taumarunui
41
Kuratau Junction
Kuratau
Omori
Tokaanu
Turangi
Raurimu
47
▲ MT TONGARIRO
National Park
▲ MT NGAURUHOE
Whakapapa
Iwikau Village
TONGARIRO
▲ MT RUAPEHU
NATIONAL
PARK
Turoa Skifield
WHANGANUI
NATIONAL
PARK
Whanganui River
Tohunga Junction
Raetihi
Ohakune
Pipiriki
Jerusalem
4
Koriniti
Kakatahi
Mangawhero River
Upokongaro
WANGANUI

Hamilton–Wanganui SH 4
325 km, 6 hours

Take SH 3 to Te Kuiti (see Hamilton–New Plymouth, Route 15). SH 4 begins 11 km south of Te Kuiti at Eight Mile Junction and proceeds through the hilly mudstone and limestone hinterland between central North Island and eastern Taranaki. The road to Taumarunui is fairly windy though always scenic (1 hour).

Taumarunui

Maori have lived on the banks of the upper Whanganui River for centuries, using the river as the major route to the coast at Wanganui. The area was virtually off limits to Europeans until the 1880s. After Europeans settled here, and before road and rail, the river remained an important supply route to Taumarunui, while the journey by paddle steamer from Wanganui became one of the country's top tourist attractions. What now takes two hours by road was a three-day journey downstream by tourist paddle steamer. Easy canoeing and jetboating on the river into Whanganui National Park remain important tourist drawcards. Among the dreary chip shops and tearooms on the main street you'll be pleased to find the fine Rivers II Café.

National Park – campground, walks

National Park settlement is just 25 minutes from Taumarunui. In this short time the landscape is transformed as it climbs from the enclosing hills of Taumarunui to the open tussock-covered plateau below Tongariro National Park's active volcanoes. Shortly before National Park, railway buffs will appreciate the Raurimu Spiral lookout at Raurimu, though even the cartographically literate will struggle to decipher the explanatory map. National Park, at the junction with SH 47 to Turangi (49 km), offers ski lodges, cafés, bars and a myriad of purchasable 'adventures'. Eivens Café offers a better coffee than you'll get at Whakapapa village, 16 km from here in Tongariro National Park.

Mt Ngaruhoe from Mt Tongariro, Tongariro National Park

Whakapapa – campground, walks, skiing

Whakapapa's park visitor centre has excellent interpretive displays covering geology, flora and fauna, and the Maori and European relationships with this landscape – now a World Heritage Area. Walking options range from 15 minutes to all day. Most renowned is the day-long crossing of Mt Tongariro. The 6 km sealed road to Iwikau Village and skifield takes you into a raw landscape of lava flows, boulder fields, tussocks and impressive vistas.

The Chateau at Whakapapa, Mt Ruapehu

Ohakune – campground, walks

If it's at all possible let the sun coat the western slopes of the volcanoes in the late afternoon or evening before you drive toward Ohakune. The vistas are magnificent. Turn off SH 4 at Tohunga Junction to reach Ohakune. In winter, Ohakune's nightclubs and bars are jammed with partying skiers. It's a quieter town in summer, but there are still several cafés open (try Utopia or Johnny's chocolate eclair shop on the main street). The 17 km drive (sealed) to Turoa skifield offers forest and alpine walks, picnicking and fine views. A park visitor centre is located at the park entrance.

Raetihi

Raetihi is an unremarkable town, with any tourism interest derived from its proximity to Ohakune and Whanganui National Park, 30 minutes west of SH 4 at Pipiriki (the last kilometres to Pipiriki are un-sealed).

Pipiriki (Whanganui National Park) – walks, picnicking, boating

Pipiriki is where most kayakers and canoeists from Taumarunui finish their journey. There's a 30-minute walk from the DoC office, though the easiest way to experience the park is by jetboat – tours can be arranged here. Colonial House, a registered historic place, doubles as an information centre. Having come this far I'd recommend the river road down the Whanganui River to Wanganui (1.5-2 hours, covered by a heritage trail brochure). It's a slow, scenic journey with river and forest scenery, pa, marae and sites sacred to Maori. Such was the spiritual and practical relationship Maori had with the river, they named virtually every corner. Jerusalem, 11 km from Pipiriki, is most commonly associated with the commune established there by the revered poet James K Baxter. The 31 km unsealed section to Koriniti is suitable for campervans. There are no shops or service stations until Upokongaro back on SH 4.

Raetihi–Wanganui

Allow 1.5 hours for the 94 km run to Wanganui on SH 4. The road is hilly and windy, traversing farmed land above the Mangawhero River much of the way. Fuel and refreshments are available at Kakatahi (33 km from Raetihi). A worthwhile diversion is to drive 3–4 km up the Whanganui river road (42 km from Kakatahi) to a highpoint overlooking the Whanganui Valley at the beginning of Aramoana Walkway.

Taumarunui–Turangi SH 41
61 km, 40 minutes

This route crosses the forested Waihaha Scenic Reserve south of Pureora Forest Park. Waituhi Lookout on the crest of the range offers excellent views across Lake Taupo and the Tongariro volcanoes. After Kuratau Junction (43 km from Taumarunui), pleasant reserves and beaches at Omori and Kuratau on the shores of Lake Taupo are a short distance off the highway. Allow time to stop at the Tokaanu hot springs, a DoC facility where you can enjoy a pleasant soak and forest walks.

Canoes on the Whanganui River

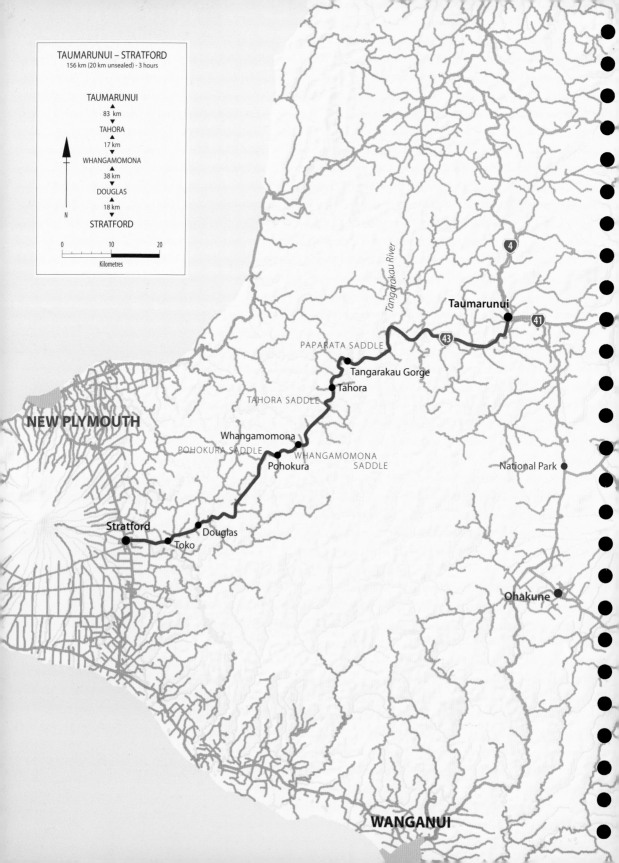

TAUMARUNUI – STRATFORD
156 km (20 km unsealed) - 3 hours

TAUMARUNUI
▲
83 km
▼
TAHORA
▲
17 km
▼
WHANGAMOMONA
▲
38 km
▼
DOUGLAS
▲
18 km
▼
STRATFORD

N

0   10   20
Kilometres

Tangarakau River

④

Taumarunui

㊶

㊸

PAPARATA SADDLE

Tangarakau Gorge

Tahora

TAHORA SADDLE

Whangamomona

POHOKURA SADDLE

WHANGAMOMONA
SADDLE

Pohokura

NEW PLYMOUTH

National Park

Stratford

Douglas

Toko

Ohakune

WANGANUI

Taumarunui–Stratford SH 43
156 km (20 km unsealed), 3 hours

This under-rated scenic drive into the hilly backblocks of Eastern Taranaki traverses three saddles, forest reserves and the beautiful Tangarakau Gorge Scenic Reserve. The highway follows a sinuous path through the hills, but despite a 20 km unsealed section is still passable in a campervan.

SH 43 is a designated heritage trail and is supported with informative panels en route and a heritage trail brochure which points out walks and places of historical import. The history of the area is absorbing, encompassing Maori resistance to European settlement, coal mining, forest clearance and establishment of farms on marginal, slip-prone land, and the building of the road and railway through here. There is no petrol for 140 km (until Toko) so fuel up at Taumarunui.

The first scenic highlight is after the Ohinepa Scenic Reserve (toilets, camping, picnicking) at Nevins Lookout about 30 km from Taumarunui. Then after crossing Paparata Saddle the road reaches the still pools of the Tangarakau Gorge Scenic Reserve. On Tahora Saddle is the perfectly located Kaieto Café with fine views from the porch across a landscape of the Tongariro volcanoes, forest remnants and farmed land slipping off the ridges. Such is the state of much of the land here you have to question the wisdom of those who cleared the forests believing the papa (mudstone) hills could sustain a monoculture. You can camp or park a campervan next to the café.

Whangamomona is the largest settlement on the route with its pub, backpackers and campground. From here SH 43 climbs to its high point, the 270 m Whangamomona Saddle. The final saddle, Pohokura, is just a few kilometres on, followed by the descent to easier travel east of Stratford.

Hill country near Taumarunui

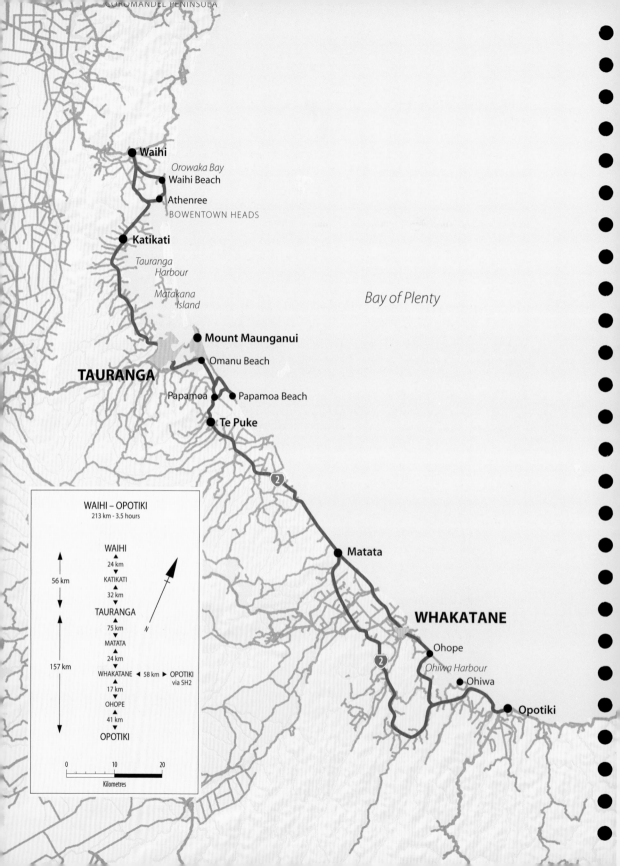

COROMANDEL PENINSULA

Waihi

Orowaka Bay
Waihi Beach

Athenree
BOWENTOWN HEADS

Katikati

*Tauranga
Harbour*

*Matakana
Island*

Bay of Plenty

● **Mount Maunganui**

Omanu Beach

Papamoa ● Papamoa Beach

● **Te Puke**

②

● **Matata**

WHAKATANE

Ohope
Ohiwa Harbour

● Ohiwa

②

Opotiki

TAURANGA

WAIHI – OPOTIKI
213 km - 3.5 hours

WAIHI
▲ 24 km ▼
KATIKATI
▲ 32 km ▼
TAURANGA
▲ 75 km ▼
MATATA
▲ 24 km ▼
WHAKATANE ◄ 58 km ► OPOTIKI
▲ 17 km ▼   via SH2
OHOPE
▲ 41 km ▼
OPOTIKI

56 km

157 km

N

0   10   20
Kilometres

Waihi–Opotiki SH 2
213 km, 3.5 hours

A drive through the hills and coastal plains of Bay of Plenty, passing resorts at Waihi Beach, Mount Maunganui, Papamoa Beach and Ohope along the way. SH 2 is a busy road which services the region's market gardening, fruitgrowing and forestry industries.

Waihi Beach – campground, swimming
Waihi Beach occupies a lengthy sweep of coast south of Waihi. Between Waihi Beach and the Bowentown Heads are safe swimming beaches, good surfing, hot pools at Athenree, camping, and a walk to Orokawa Bay at the north end of the beach.

The turnoff to Waihi Beach is 4 km from Waihi. Back on SH 2 the road skirts Tauranga Harbour through to Katikati, Tauranga and Mount Maunganui. Look for the Twickenham Café and gardens on the northern outskirts of Katikati which makes yummy cakes and excellent coffee. North of Tauranga are a number of wineries including the Morton Estate winery and café.

Mount Maunganui – campground, walks, swimming
Mount Maunganui (turn off SH 2 at Omanu Beach) has become a rather glitzy resort with any number of beachfront cafés. The beach is splendid while walks on the Mount offer outstanding coastal views over Tauranga Harbour, Matakana Island and the Bay of Plenty.

Mount Maunganui

Papamoa Beach – campground, swimming
A rapidly developing resort village and retirement haven, complete with shopping mall. On the beachfront is the nicely situated campground and the Blue Bijou café.

Whakatane/Ohope
From Papamoa Beach return to SH 2 and drive through Te Puke to Whakatane (45 minutes, turn off SH 2 at Matata). The more scenic and quicker route to Opotiki is through Ohope resort and around Ohiwa Harbour. Just past Ohope is the easy 1 hour walk around the Tauwhare Pa, a once fortified village, which overlooks Ohiwa Harbour. The pa has a fascinating history, and offers fine views, and birdwatching.

Opotiki – campground, walks, swimming
Arching groves of pohutukawa enfold the highway as it nears Opotiki. A few minutes from the town on a roadside reserve is the arresting carving *Te Ara Ki Te Tairawhiti*, the 'Pathway to the Sunrise' by artist Heke Collier, whose carvings are also found on Opotiki's main street. Those who require sustenance should try the Hot Bread Shop and Illy Café at 43 St John St (where it intersects with SH 2).

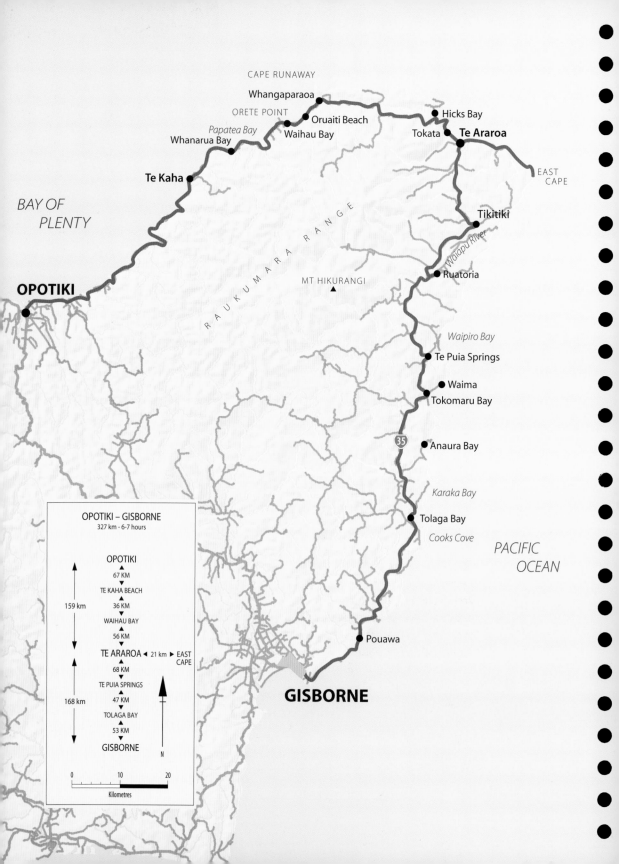

CAPE RUNAWAY

Whangaparaoa

ORETE POINT

Papatea Bay
Oruaiti Beach
Waihau Bay

Whanarua Bay

Hicks Bay

Tokata   **Te Araroa**

EAST
CAPE

Te Kaha

*BAY OF
PLENTY*

Tikitiki

Waiapu River

OPOTIKI

Ruatoria

RAUKUMARA RANGE

MT HIKURANGI

Waipiro Bay

Te Puia Springs

Waima
Tokomaru Bay

35   Anaura Bay

Karaka Bay

Tolaga Bay

Cooks Cove

*PACIFIC
OCEAN*

Pouawa

GISBORNE

OPOTIKI – GISBORNE
327 km - 6-7 hours

OPOTIKI
▲
67 KM
▼
TE KAHA BEACH
▲
36 KM
159 km   ▼
WAIHAU BAY
▲
56 KM
▼
TE ARAROA ◄ 21 km ► EAST
▲   CAPE
68 KM
▼
TE PUIA SPRINGS
168 km   ▲
47 KM
▼
TOLAGA BAY
▲
53 KM
▼
GISBORNE

N

0   10   20

Kilometres

Opotiki–Gisborne SH 35
327 km, 6–7 hours

The drive around East Cape from Opotiki to Gisborne is one of the most memorable in New Zealand. Much of the Cape's appeal comes from resilient Maori communities who have maintained links with their culture, history and landscape. Evidence of this is everywhere in the numerous marae with their distinctive carved or painted wharenui (meeting houses), and in their memorials and schools.

European history is another distinctive feature of the region. This history is recounted in numerous places: the Cook Landing Site National Historic Reserve in Gisborne, the wharf at Tolaga Bay, and the beautiful Anglican Church at Tikitiki in which the melding of European and Maori culture is evocatively illustrated.

Opotiki–Whangaparaoa 118 km
From Opotiki SH 35 more or less hugs the Bay of Plenty coast as far as Whangaparaoa, in places cutting high onto bluffs and hills allowing views of the spectacular land and seascape and into the forested Raukumara hinterland. Beaches and campgrounds reinforce the holiday feel of this coastal section of the highway where places to camp, swim, fish, snorkel, dive, picnic or go horse trekking are many.

Te Kaha – campground, swimming, fishing
Once a whaling village, Te Kaha is these days a popular holiday destination with safe swimming and fishing, a splendid meeting house and what remains of a redoubt at Te Kaha Tukaki marae.

Whanarua Bay – campground, picnicking, swimming, fishing
Claimed to have its own microclimate, the bay's central attractions are its secluded beaches, swimming and fishing, and coastal views from Karirangi Hill including White Island.

Waihau Bay – campground, picnicking, swimming, fishing
Another popular destination, here an espresso machine at the camp store and café makes a lone stand on a route where fish and chip culture is paramount. The nearby Oruaiti Beach is considered the best on this stretch. At Orete Point near the Waihau Bay Lodge (really just a flash pub) is a plaque commemorating the fact that in 1897 'nothing happened'.

Lighthouse, East Cape (photo Dave Chowdhury)

Whangaparaoa

Steeped in Maori history, Whangaparaoa has a reinstated pa and meeting house open to visitors, while guided historic tours of the area over Maori land are also offered. The beach at Whangaparaoa Bay is said to be where the Tainui and Arawa canoes landed with their cargo of colonisers from Hawaiiki circa 1350 AD.

Whangaparaoa–Gisborne 209 km

South of Cape Runaway is the Ngati Porou tribal area. From Whangaparaoa, SH 35 remains inland for much of the route to Gisborne, the exceptions being sections from Hicks Bay to Te Araroa and Pouawa to Gisborne.

Hicks Bay

Hicks Bay occupies an important place in the history of the Ngati Porou, whose people have lived here for up to 1000 years. There are many historic sites and excavated fortifications. Tuwhakairiora meeting house, 'one of the finest in the East Cape', was named for a famous warrior to whom the area's original families trace their lineage. St Barnabas Church (1979) in the marae grounds is embellished with Maori art and exhibits a marriage of traditional and recent architecture.

Te Araroa

From Hicks Bay the road presents excellent views over the coast before the descent to the Tokata Flats where there is a holiday park. Soon after is the coastal settlement of Te Araroa. What is claimed to be the country's oldest (600 years) and largest pohutukawa (named Te Waha-o-Rerekohu) stands on the edge of Hinerupe marae on the beach front.

East Cape Lighthouse – walk

From Te Araroa you can drive to New Zealand's most easterly point and climb the several hundred steps to the East Cape lighthouse atop Otiki Hill (42 km return, mostly unsealed, 20 minutes one way. Watch out for wandering stock and horses). The track crosses Ngati Porou land, and although permission isn't required, a $2 koha (donation) is requested.

Tikitiki

Between Te Araroa and Tikitiki, SH 35 traverses rural and forest landscapes and climbs high onto a ridge offering views of the Raukumara Range and the Waiapu Mountains – the sacred peaks of the Ngati Porou – the highest and most important of these being Mt Hikurangi (1752 m). On a fine day Hikurangi can be seen from many places between Tikitiki and Te Puia.

Tikitiki is on the north bank of the Waiapu River and is where the beautiful St Mary's Church is located. Like Hicks Bay, excavated fortifications dating to the 1860 land wars are found on the hill above the settlement.

Ruatoria

Nineteen kilometres further is Ruatoria, East Cape's largest settlement which is dominated by views of Mt Hikurangi and nearby peaks. For local kai, the chefs at the Blue Boar Tavern & Mountain View Café, near the turnoff to Ruatoria, will prepare paua burgers and delicious ice-cream sundaes.

South of Ruatoria, enquire at the Te Puia Springs hotel about a dip in the hot springs.

Tokomaru Bay – swimming

The welcoming sweep of Tokomaru Bay is reached 11 km from Te Puia. As well as catering for holi-daymakers with a range of accommodation and services, Tokomaru Bay is a favoured haunt of fish-ers and local artists and crafts people. There is a safe beach, and the Te Puka Tavern on the road east towards Waima is just a few metres from the sea. There are four marae at the bay including Pakirikiri marae (1934) which has a large carved meeting house.

Memorial Hall, Ruatoria

Anaura Bay – campground, walks

From Tokomaru Bay the road returns inland and climbs high through prime East Cape sheep farming country. Anaura Bay, a 7 km diversion from SH 35 about 22 km from Tokomaru Bay, has a campground and a 3.5 km coastal walkway through farmland and forest.

Tolaga Bay – walks

Tolaga Bay (36 km from Tokomaru Bay, 53 km from Gisborne) is renowned for the 700 metre concrete jetty at the bay's southern end. Completed in 1929, the jetty serviced coastal shipping until 1967. Though in need of restoration the jetty is still used by recreational fishers or those who want a stroll. Near the wharf is the Cooks Cove walkway (allow 2–3 hours) through farm and forest and along cliff tops to a lookout, the Hole in the Wall and Cooks Cove itself. A memorial records the visit of Captain Cook to Tolaga Bay in October 1769.

Pouawa–Gisborne

At Pouawa is the Te Tapuwae O Rongokako marine reserve which is administered by the Department of Conservation, local iwi, and recreational and commercial fishers. Pouawa is a popular free-camping, swimming and diving area, though fishing is banned in the reserve. The drive to Gisborne follows the Pacific coast through several small settlements and past formal and informal camping sites on the edge of surf and swimming beaches.

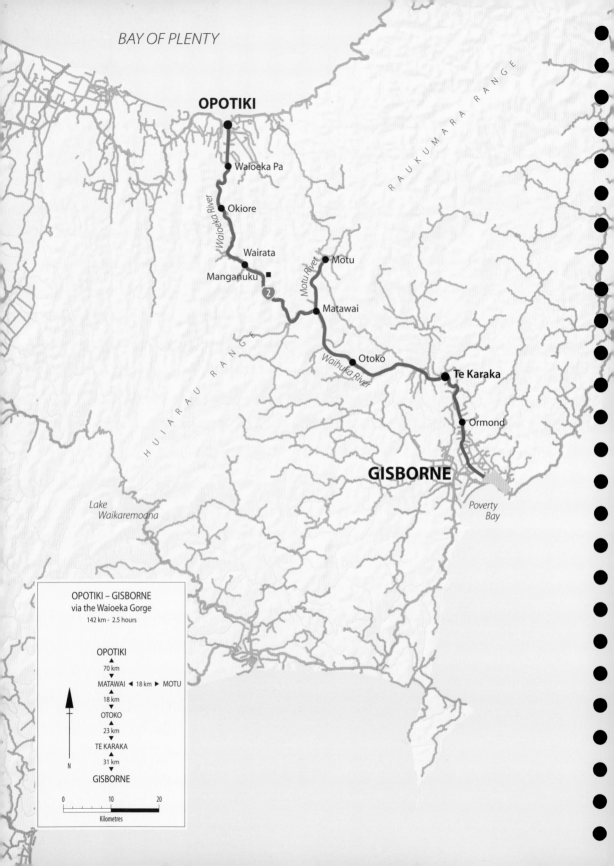

BAY OF PLENTY

OPOTIKI

Waioeka Pa

Okiore

Waioeka River

Wairata

Manganuku

Motu

Motu River

Matawai

Otoko

Waihuka River

Te Karaka

Ormond

GISBORNE

RAUKUMARA RANGE

HUIARAU RANGE

Lake Waikaremoana

Poverty Bay

OPOTIKI – GISBORNE
via the Waioeka Gorge
142 km - 2.5 hours

OPOTIKI
▲
70 km
▼
MATAWAI ◄ 18 km ► MOTU
▲
18 km
▼
OTOKO
▲
23 km
▼
TE KARAKA
▲
31 km
▼
GISBORNE

N

0   10   20
Kilometres

Opotiki–Gisborne via the Waioeka Gorge SH 2

142 km, 2.5 hours , sealed

The highlight of this route is the 45 km Waioeka Gorge which begins 14 kilometres south of Opotiki.

Waioeka Gorge

At the entrance to the gorge is the excellent Gorge in the Gorge Café and craft shop whose owners also run kayak trips on the Waioeka River.

Into the gorge and following the Waioeka River, the road winds between the steep forested flanks of the Huiarau and Raukumara ranges. Three kilometres from the café is the Waioeka nature trail, a worthwhile and easy 15-minute interpreted forest walk.

Seven kilometres further is the start of the Tauranga Track where a short walk leads to a recently restored historic suspension bridge. The Manganuku campground (DoC), 47 km from Opotiki, has toilets and barbecue sites, and is the start of a couple of longer tramping routes.

Matawai – campground

After the campground the highway leaves the gorge and ascends Traffords Hill then crosses into the upper reaches of the Motu River to Matawai village. The 18 km diversion north from Matawai along a sealed road to Motu is of interest for those interested in horsetrekking, mountain-biking, walking, rafting and fishing. The easy Whinray Reserve Bush Walk to Motu Falls is recommended.

Motu River

Te Karaka

Back on SH 2 the journey to Gisborne follows the Waihuka River, passing Otoko (where you can take a walk along the Otoko Walkway – all that remains of the old Moutohora railway link to Gisborne) and Te Karaka on the Poverty Bay river flats.

Ormond

Towards Ormond you enter Gisborne's prosperous horticultural and wine-growing area. Along this stretch is the so-called 'slope of gold' chardonnay-growing area. A number of wineries are located hereabouts including Longbush, TW, Acton Estate and the Pouparae Park boutique winery. Wine tastings at these wineries are by appointment only. Montana's wines can be tasted at their shop on Lyttons Rd in Gisborne. (See Gisborne– Wairoa, Route 23 for locations of other wineries.)

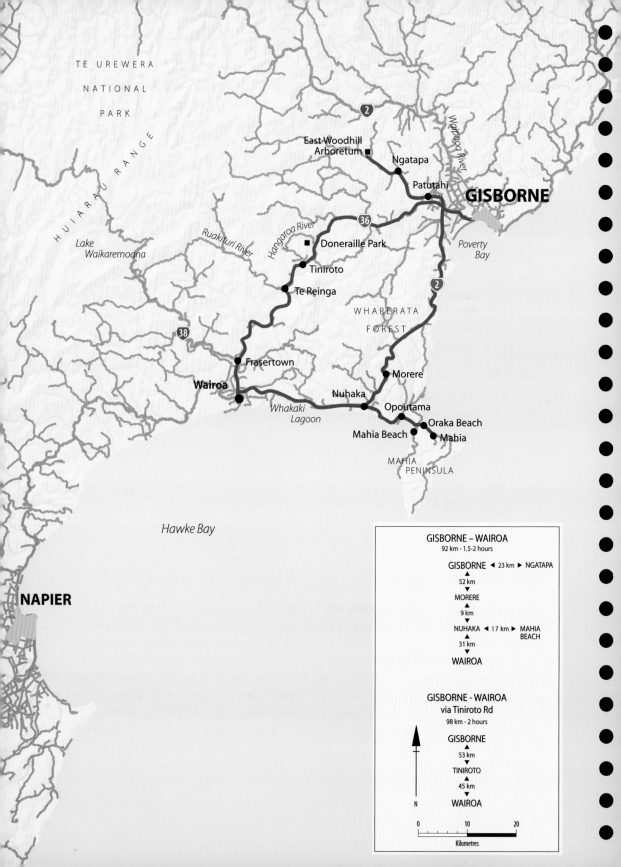

TE UREWERA

NATIONAL

PARK

HUIARAU RANGE

Lake Waikaremoana

Ruakituri River

Hangaroa River

East Woodhill Arboretum ■

Ngatapa

Patutahi

GISBORNE

Waipaoa River

36

Doneraille Park ■

Tiniroto

Te Reinga

Poverty Bay

WHARERATA FOREST

38

Frasertown

Morere

Wairoa

Nuhaka

Opoutama

Whakaki Lagoon

Oraka Beach

Mahia Beach

Mahia

MAHIA PENINSULA

Hawke Bay

NAPIER

GISBORNE – WAIROA
92 km - 1.5-2 hours

GISBORNE ◄ 23 km ► NGATAPA

▲ 52 km ▼

MORERE

▲ 9 km ▼

NUHAKA ◄ 17 km ► MAHIA BEACH

▲ 31 km ▼

WAIROA

GISBORNE - WAIROA
via Tiniroto Rd
98 km - 2 hours

GISBORNE

▲ 53 km ▼

TINIROTO

▲ 45 km ▼

WAIROA

N

0   10   20

Kilometres

Gisborne–Wairoa SH 2
92 km, 1.5–2 hours

From Gisborne SH 2 enters the Poverty Bay flats through the Matawhero winegrowing area, and heads south towards the large Wharerata pine plantation and Mahia Peninsula.

About 2 km towards Wairoa and Napier from the SH 2 turnoff to Opotiki is Riverpoint Rd at the end of which is the Matawhero vineyard and the Colosseum Café. Just over the Waipaoa River a right turn at the roundabout onto Patutahi/Ngatapa Rd leads to the Shalimar Estate vineyard. Highly recommended is to continue on this road past Ngatapa to the internationally renowned East Woodhill Arboretum (35 km from Gisborne, sealed road).

 Morere – campground, walks
Morere hot springs 52 km from Gisborne at the south end of Wharerata forest is an attractively laid out spa in a 200 ha native forest reserve. As well as a variety of public and private thermal pools, the reserve has a number of forest walks. A great place for a pause.

 Mahia Peninsula – campgrounds, walks, surfing, swimming
At Nuhaka is the turnoff to the Mahia Peninsula, a very popular surfing, swimming and holiday destination. Mahia Beach settlement is 17 km from Nuhaka at the south end of Opoutama Beach. The drive there is sealed and offers fine views along the peninsula, and is particularly dramatic in the evenings when a strong swell is running and low sun lights the clifflines. Beyond Mahia Beach the sealed road, now somewhat narrower, continues to Oraka Beach and Mahia on the peninsula's eastern side.

Back on SH 2 it's a straight run west past Whakaki lagoon into Wairoa.

Gisborne–Wairoa via Tiniroto SH 6 (The Tiniroto Road)
98 km, 1.5–2 hours

This alternative route to SH 2 winds through the hilly and often spectacular rural hinterland west of Gisborne. The road is sealed and narrow in places. Highlights include Doneraille Park (47 km from Gisborne), a forest reserve next to the Hangaroa River, with safe swimming, a campground and toilets. Three kilometres from Tiniroto is Hackfalls Arboretum which has a large collection of oaks, poplars and maples.

Te Reinga Falls is in one of the few scraps of native forest left in the area a short distance along Ruakituri Valley Rd from Te Reinga. The impressive 18 m falls tumble over a sandstone bluff into a narrow slot which the nimble-footed can get a better view of from an informal track which descends to a rock platform. Slippery when wet! Frasertown (91 km from Gisborne, 7 km from Wairoa) is a small town at the junction with SH 38 which leads to Te Urewera National Park. (See Rotorua–Wairoa, Route 26).

TE UREWERA

NATIONAL

PARK

H U I A R A U   R A N G E

Lake
Waikaremoana

36

GISBORNE

Poverty
Bay

2

38

Wairoa

Whakaki
Lagoon

BOUNDARY
STREAM
SCENIC
RESERVE

2

MAHIA
PENINSULA

Tutira

Lake Tutira

TANGOIO
FOREST

Hawke Bay

Tangoio

NAPIER

WAIROA – NAPIER
119 km - 2 hours

WAIROA
▲
75 km
▼
TUTIRA
▲
21 km
▼
TANGOIO
▲
23 km
▼
NAPIER

N

0   10   20

Kilometres

Wairoa–Napier SH 2
119 km, 2 hours

This route traverses the hilly rural hinterland between Wairoa and Napier, passing several small settlements and high points with views toward Hawke Bay. Closer to Napier are several interesting reserves: Lake Tutira, White Pine Bush and Tangoio.

Lake Tutira – picnicking, swimming, walks, fishing
Seventy-five kilometres from Wairoa, the Lake Tutira wildlife refuge and its environs occupies a special place in New Zealand conservation history thanks to the efforts of a pioneer farmer and conservationist Herbert Guthrie Smith. A carpark at the southern end provides access to a pleasant picnic site and the start of several walking tracks.

Boundary Stream Scenic Reserve – walks
Boundary Stream, a 700 ha forest remnant north of Tutira (75 km from Wairoa) is one of six 'mainland islands' established by the Department of Conservation. The 'mainland island' concept involves a determined effort to reduce introduced pests such as rats, stoats and possums to enable native plants and animals to recover, and even allow the re-introduction of endangered species that might otherwise only survive on islands offshore. Although such islands involve a long range view, in just a few years there are encouraging signs that birdlife and forest species are staging a recovery at Boundary Stream. To reach the reserve, turn onto Matahorua Rd by the Tutira store. For an interesting walk, take the lefthand fork (about 6 km from the store) onto Pohukura Rd and drive to the Kamahi Loop track, a 2 hour loop through a varied lowland podocarp and kamahi forest.

White Pine Bush/ Tangoio Falls – picnicking, walks
A 19 ha forest remnant 96 km from Wairoa features tall kahikatea (white pine) and other rainforest trees that once covered the rest of the surrounding landscape. A 30-minute loop through the forest (best done anticlockwise) is accessible to wheelchairs. Two kilometres on is the Tangoio Falls Scenic Reserve where there is a 15-minute forest walk to Te Ana Falls.

Kahikatea trees

From here SH 2 winds through pine forest to reach the Hawke Bay coastline just past Tangoio settlement, 23 km from Napier.

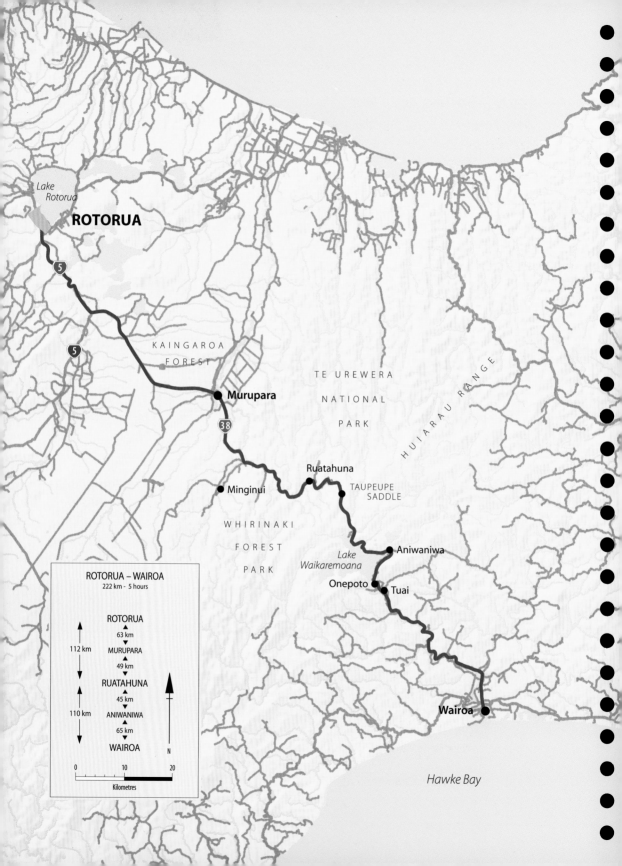

Lake Rotorua

ROTORUA

5

5

KAINGAROA
FOREST

● **Murupara**

38

● Minginui

Ruatahuna
●

TE UREWERA

NATIONAL

PARK

TAUPEUPE
SADDLE

WHIRINAKI

FOREST

Lake
Waikaremoana

● **Aniwaniwa**

PARK

Onepoto ●   ● **Tuai**

HUIARAU RANGE

Wairoa ●

Hawke Bay

ROTORUA – WAIROA
222 km - 5 hours

ROTORUA
▲
▼ 63 km
MURUPARA
112 km   ▲
▼ 49 km
RUATAHUNA
▲
▼ 45 km
ANIWANIWA
110 km   ▲
▼ 65 km
WAIROA

N

0   10   20

Kilometres

Rotorua–Waikaremoana–Wairoa
SH 5, 38 and 120 km of unsealed road
222 km, 5 hours

On the plus side, the road to Lake Waikaremoana ranks as one of the most scenic in this book, in-volving, by my estimation, the longest forest drive in New Zealand – the 102 km between Murupara and Onepoto at Lake Waikaremoana in Te Urewera National Park. The area is remote, covered in dense podocarp and beech forest, and resounds with Maori history and culture. On the negative, the route is mostly unsealed and often narrow, locals drive it too fast, and unfortunately some tourists can't handle the hazards. That said, by New Zealand standards of unsealed roads, it rates as one of the better ones for road surface. Campervans can make the journey, but check your insurance first (as should drivers of all rentals).

From Rotorua take SH 5 to the SH 38 junction (26 km) and proceed through Kaingaroa Forest to Murupara (1 hour).

Murupara
Visit the DoC office here for information on the road, camping sites, and walks. Allow 2 hours to reach Aniwaniwa (excluding sightseeing!) from Murupara. Beyond Murupara the road approaches the barrier of hills formed by the Te Urewera ranges, passing a sign indicating a winding road for a mere 120 km. The tarmac ends not far past the turnoff to Minginui and Whirinaki Forest Park (an outstanding podocarp reserve with a roadend campground and many rewarding forest walks).

Ruatahuna
A farming locality cleared from the forest, and traditional centre of the Tuhoe people who have inhabited the Te Urewera ranges for hundreds of years. Whole families on horseback driving stock is a diverting and not uncommon sight around these parts. From Ruatahuna the road climbs to Papiiora Ridge with fine views of ranges and forest. The road then crosses Taupeupe Saddle (919 m) on the crest of the Huiarau Range from where the rivers and the road drop toward the northern arm of Lake Waikaremoana.

Aniwaniwa Visitor Centre – campground, walks
The descent to and drive around the lake to Aniwaniwa is one of increasingly beautiful vistas. There are several roadside camp-ing sites on this section. At Aniwaniwa, the national park infor-mation centre provides an absorbing interpretation of the natu-ral and cultural values of this region. From the visitor centre the road continues along the eastern shore until the forest abruptly ends and the road descends steeply to Tuai. At Tuai is the incon-gruous Rangers Café and Bar (saddles on bar stools, yee-ha) with adjacent accommodation and campsites.

Beech forest, Te Urewera National Park

Allow 1 hour to Wairoa from Tuai.

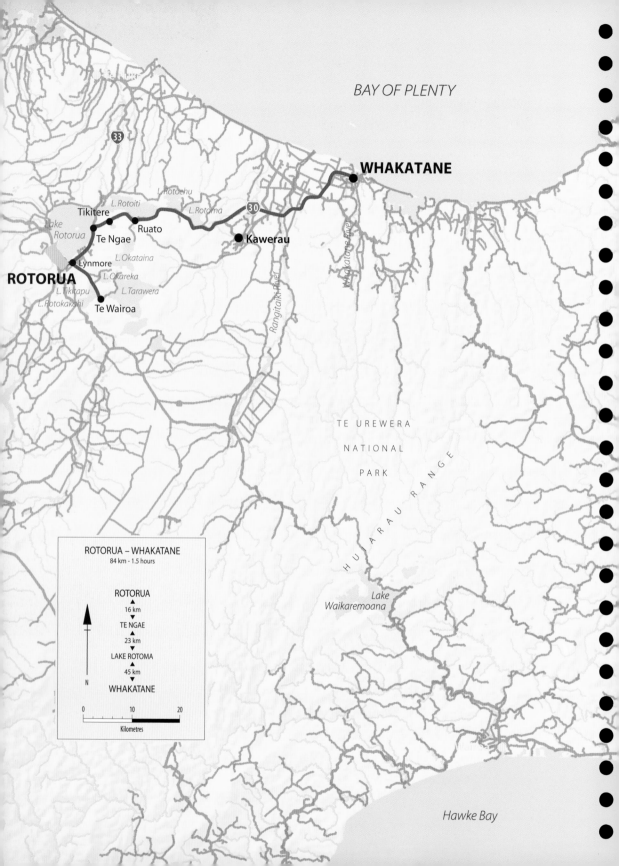

BAY OF PLENTY

WHAKATANE

L. Rotoehu
L. Rotoiti
L. Rotoma
Tikitere
Ruato
33
30
Te Ngae
Kawerau
Lake Rotorua
L. Okataina
Lynmore
L. Okareka
ROTORUA
L. Tikitapu
L. Tarawera
L. Rotokakahi
Te Wairoa

Rangitaiki River
Whakatane River

TE UREWERA

NATIONAL

PARK

HUIARAU RANGE

Lake Waikaremoana

ROTORUA – WHAKATANE
84 km - 1.5 hours

ROTORUA
▲
16 km
▼
TE NGAE
▲
23 km
▼
LAKE ROTOMA
▲
45 km
▼
WHAKATANE

N

0   10   20
Kilometres

Hawke Bay

Rotorua–Whakatane SH 30
84 km, 1.5 hours

The string of beautiful lakes between Rotorua and Whakatane are the highlights of this drive. You could spend any amount of time swimming, picnicking, fishing, boating or walking at these lakes which also have high natural and cultural values.

 Lakes Okareka, Tikitapu, Rotokakahi & Tarawera – campground, walks, water recreation
This sequence of lakes is reached by turning off SH 30 at Lynmore, 3 km from Rotorua by Whakarewarewa Forest Park. The lakes are well signposted and are reached along sealed roads. Lakes Tikitapu and Okareka are both 11 km from Rotorua. Tikitapu has a campground and store and at its southern end is a viewpoint which also overlooks Rotokakahi. Lake Okareka offers picnicking in a quiet reserve. The Te Wairoa buried village is reached shortly before Lake Tarawera after a pleasant forested drive. Here there is a café, museum and tours of the village.

Back on SH 30, the route skirts the eastern shores of Lake Rotorua then turns inland towards Lake Rotoiti. (SH 33 to Te Puke turns off at Te Ngae – allow 40 minutes).

 Tikitere (Hells Gate Thermal Reserve) – walks, picnicking
Not far from Te Ngae is this iwi-owned thermal reserve, the most active thermal area in the region. Rotorua's only mud volcano and the largest hot waterfall in this hemisphere are among its attractions.

 Lakes Rotoiti, Rotoehu, Okataina & Rotoma – walks, picnicking, water recreation
A picnic area at the eastern end of Lake Rotoiti also has an easy track to the more secluded Lake Rotoehu. Halfway around Lake Rotoiti at Ruato is the turnoff to Lake Okataina, perhaps the prettiest of the lakes with its native forest surrounds. There are a number of short forest walks from the road end. There is a campground at Lake Rotoma.

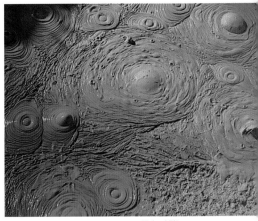

Mud pool, Tikitere

From Rotoma, SH 30 descends through native forests and pine plantations, past the loop road to Kawerau, and onto the Rangitaiki River plains to Whakatane.

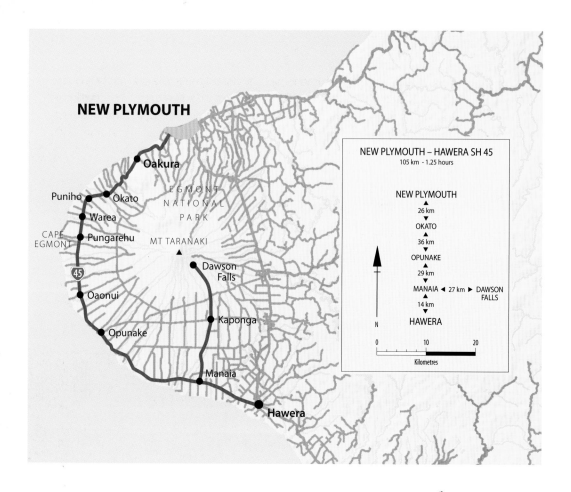

NEW PLYMOUTH

Oakura

Puniho   Okato

Warea

CAPE
EGMONT   Pungarehu

EGMONT
NATIONAL
PARK

MT TARANAKI

Dawson
Falls

45

Oaonui

Opunake

Kaponga

Manaia

Hawera

NEW PLYMOUTH – HAWERA SH 45
105 km - 1.25 hours

NEW PLYMOUTH
▲
26 km
▼
OKATO
▲
36 km
▼
OPUNAKE
▲
29 km
▼
MANAIA ◄ 27 km ► DAWSON
▲   FALLS
14 km
▼
HAWERA

N

0   10   20
Kilometres

New Plymouth–Hawera via SH 45
105 km, 1.25 hours

The 'Surf Highway', as it's been dubbed by tourism pundits, so rarely touches the coast that even the worst predictions of climate scientists won't bring out this promise. Cynicism aside, this is a great scenic drive around the western side of Mt Taranaki, which provides access to some top surfing beaches if you have time to drive down a side road. There's fuel at most localities, but don't expect any culinary highlights until Hawera.

Oakura – campground
Oakura, 15 km from New Plymouth, is Taranaki's most popular beach resort, with a family friendly beach, excellent swimming and surfing, picnic sites and patrolled swimming areas.

Beaches beyond here are wilder and more remote and are reached via side roads signposted as you drive through Okato, Puniho, Warea and Pungarehu. There's fuel and/or a store at these places, as well as many relic dairy factories from days before amalgamations and the rise of Hawera's Kiwi Dairy Factory. The curious hillocks either side of the road are the congealed lahars (mudflows) from past eruptions of the omnipresent volcano to the east. Sunset on the mountain viewed from Cape Egmont lighthouse, 6 km west of Pungarehu is a highlight. A road just before Pungarehu leads to Parihaka, site of the world's first passive resistance movement against colonial forces. At Oaonui is the Maui gas production factory, the onshore facility where gas piped ashore from the South Taranaki Bight is processed.

Opunake – campground, walks
Opunake's Middleton Bay features a clifftop walking track and lookout over the coast. There's a popular beachfront campground and safe swimming from the beach.

Manaia
The main reason to note Manaia is the turn, at the band rotunda roundabout, to Dawson Falls in Egmont National Park. (It's possible to reach Dawson Falls by taking any one of the quieter backroads that criss-cross Mt Taranaki's ringplain from SH 45).

Dawson Falls/Mt Taranaki – walks
Dawson Falls is 20 minutes by a good road from Manaia, past the Kapuni natural gas production facility and Kaponga village (fuel). Dawson Falls has luxury and backpacker accommodation, a park visitor centre and a number of short walks and longer excursions on the flanks of Mt Taranaki. Recommended short walks are those to Wilkies Pools and to Dawson Falls.

Mt Taranaki from New Plymouth

Hawera
Distinguished by its impressive 1906 water tower, Hawera has many other notable historic buildings (a self-guide brochure on these is available from the visitor centre below the tower) and the widely acclaimed Tawhiti Museum – considered one of the country's best private museums (café). One of the museum's displays is a re-creation of the huge Turuturu Mokai pa which is the focal point of the nearby historic reserve on Turuturu Rd. A good coffee is to be had at The Café on Princes St, next to the Post Office.

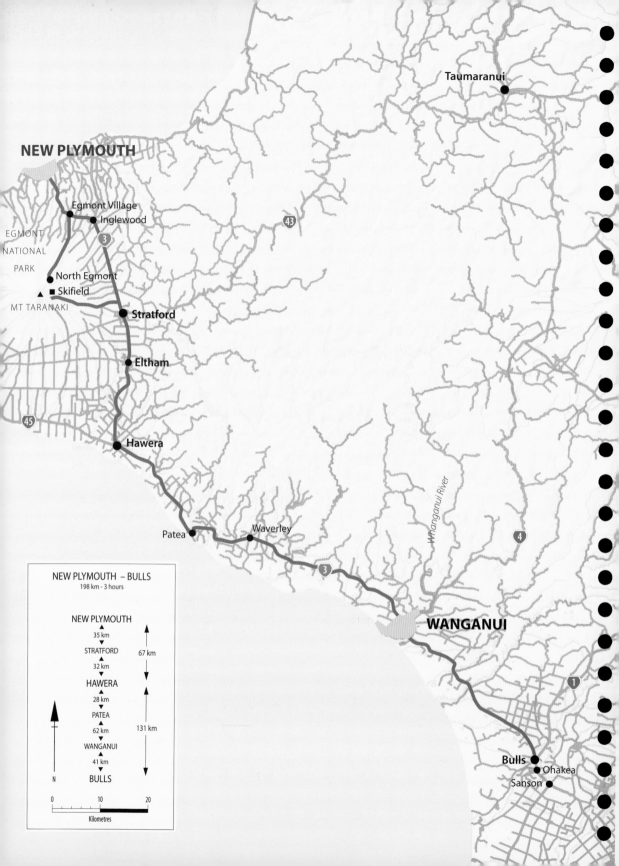

Taumaranui

NEW PLYMOUTH

Egmont Village
Inglewood

EGMONT
NATIONAL
PARK

3

North Egmont
Skifield

MT TARANAKI

Stratford

Eltham

45

Hawera

Patea
Waverley

3

Whanganui River

4

WANGANUI

NEW PLYMOUTH – BULLS
198 km - 3 hours

NEW PLYMOUTH
▲
35 km
▼
STRATFORD
▲   67 km
32 km
▼
HAWERA
▲
28 km
▼
PATEA
▲   131 km
62 km
▼
WANGANUI
▲
41 km
▼
BULLS

N

0   10   20
Kilometres

Bulls
Ohakea
Sanson

1

New Plymouth–Bulls SH 3
198 km, 3 hours

This is the main touring route south from New Plymouth, across the ringplain formed by Mt Taranaki, and then along coastal plains, dunelands and hill country to Bulls. With numerous towns, small settlements and the city of Wanganui en route, there is no lack of facilities for travellers.

On the outskirts of New Plymouth is the Meeting of the Waters Scenic Reserve, a good place for a picnic, walks in native forest and swimming. Further down the road at Egmont Village (12 km from New Plymouth) is the excellent Café 1281 and the turnoff to North Egmont Visitor Centre in Egmont National Park.

North Egmont, Mt Taranaki – walks
Twenty minutes from Egmont Village, after a narrow winding drive through the forests of Egmont National Park, the road emerges at the bushline at North Egmont. There is an excellent park visitor centre and café here, several forest and alpine walks and fine views of the surrounds and the North Taranaki coast.

Stratford – walks
Back on SH 3, kids would no doubt enjoy the toy factory at Inglewood, otherwise it's a straight run through to Stratford. Signposted at the northern end of the town is the Pembroke Rd access to East Egmont. The sealed road (access to Manganui Skifield) climbs well beyond the forest edge to the Stratford Plateau (1100 m) for commanding views of the region, coastline, and on a clear day the central North Island volcanoes. Back down the mountain there's a shop at the mountain house and forest walks.

Just south of Stratford is the Taranaki Pioneer Village, a replica village which now stands alongside a recently opened Maori arts and crafts venture. Visitors can view artists at work, and purchase or commission new work – all of which bear the three feathers of peace insignia of the pacifist chief Te Whiti of Parihaka (see Route 28).

Eltham – walks
Eltham, like Hawera (see Route 28), has many historic buildings, some of which are over 100 years old. You can see these for yourself by picking up the *Historic Eltham* brochure from any of the Taranaki visitor centres and following the self-guided heritage walk. Speciality cheeses produced by the local industry can be tasted and bought from the 'Cheese Bar' on Bridge St.

Hawera (see also Route 28)
Three kilometres south of Hawera is the largest dairy factory in the Southern Hemisphere, run by the Kiwi Cooperative Dairy Company. Tours of the factory are not possible, however the adjacent Dairylands Visitor Centre and museum is surprisingly good value. Taranaki is first and foremost dairying country and Dairylands is the place to learn more about this industry, with its interactive displays, and even a simulated milk tanker ride in a full size model tanker! Kids love it. There's a café here too.

Bulls

Sanson

Rangitikei River

① 1

Himatangi Beach

Manawatu River

Foxton Beach   Foxton

LEVIN

Otaki

Kapiti Island

Waikanae

Paraparaumu

Paekakariki

② 2

WELLINGTON

BULLS – WELLINGTON
151 km - 2 hours

BULLS
▲
41 km
▼
FOXTON
▲
20 km
▼
LEVIN
▲
21 km
▼
OTAKI
▲
10 km
▼
WAIKANAE
▲
59 km
▼
WELLINGTON

N

0   10   20
Kilometres

Hawera–Wanganui

Allow an hour between Wanganui and Hawera, a trip which passes through Patea and Waverley townships and many small country settlements. The drive along coastal plains and hill country is pleasant enough. Fuel and refreshments are readily available.

Wanganui

Wanganui is a river city with a rich history of Maori and European settlement particularly when the Whanganui River was the main route to the central North Island. The regional museum, Virginia Lake on Wanganui's northwestern outskirts, the Sarjeant Art Gallery and Moutoa Gardens on the banks of the Whanganui River provide reasons to take a break here. From Wanganui SH 4 (the Parapara road) leads north to Tongariro National Park.

Bulls

Bulls, at the junction of SH 1 (Taupo) and SH 3 (about 40 minutes from Wanganui) is well-known for its antique/curio shops and the Ohakea Air Force Museum near Sanson. The Windmill Café is a recommended waypoint here.

Bulls–Wellington SH 1
151 km, 2 hours

Traffic is noticeably heavier beyond Bulls, particularly at weekends. South of Sanson on the coastal plains between the Rangitikei and Manawatu rivers is the lengthy Foxton straight, notorious for speeding drivers. Highlights of the drive are beach settlements at Himatangi and Foxton, and closer to Wellington on the Kapiti Coast, at Otaki, Waikanae, Paraparaumu and Paekakariki. Try Foxton's Laughing Fox Café for a refresher after the straight.

Sunset, Kapiti coast

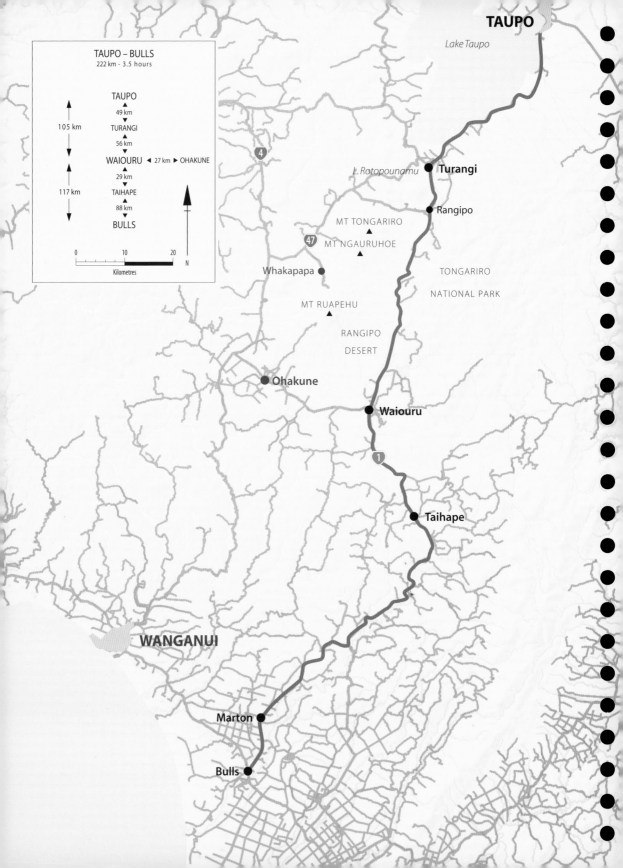

TAUPO

Lake Taupo

TAUPO – BULLS
222 km - 3.5 hours

TAUPO
▲
49 km
▼
TURANGI
▲
56 km
▼
WAIOURU ◄ 27 km ► OHAKUNE
▲
29 km
▼
TAIHAPE
▲
88 km
▼
BULLS

105 km

117 km

0   10   20
Kilometres

N

④

L. Rotopounamu ● **Turangi**

● Rangipo

MT TONGARIRO ▲

㊽ MT NGAURUHOE ▲

Whakapapa ●

TONGARIRO

NATIONAL PARK

MT RUAPEHU ▲

RANGIPO

DESERT

Ohakune ●

● **Waiouru**

①

● Taihape

WANGANUI

Marton ●

Bulls ●

Taupo–Bulls SH 1
222 km, 3.5 hours

The scenic highlights of this drive are provided by the 105 km around Lake Taupo and along the Desert Road past the Tongariro volcanoes to Waiouru. Beyond here interest pales unless you've a penchant for rural scenery. Being the main North Island highway, the road is busy, and fuel and refreshments are available from most centres.

Turangi – campground, walks
The road to Turangi stays close to the lakeshore most of the way, with many beaches and picnic sites. Turangi has a very good information centre, and fish and chip fans should try a legendary hamburger from Grand Central Fry on Ohuanga Rd – no need to order chips. SH 47 between Turangi and National Park offers excellent views of the Tongariro volcanoes. The turnoff to Whakapapa (see Hamilton–Wanganui, Route 17) is 40 km from Turangi. A number of short walks off SH 47 are covered by a DoC brochure. The Lake Rotopounamu forest walk 11 km from Turangi is recommended for its picnic sites and swimming.

The Desert Road
Between Turangi and Waiouru SH 1 crosses the Rangipo Desert. The mountain scenery is outstanding (though compromised by power pylons), best experienced in the morning when the volcanoes are lit by the sun. In winter the road can be closed by snowfall.

Waiouru
Until the Waiouru Army Museum was opened, there wasn't a lot here for visitors. The museum employs audio-visual presentations and static displays of military hardware and photography to recount New Zealand's military history from nineteenth century land wars to contemporary UN peacekeeping. Far from glorifying the military, the account is often moving. Waiouru's best café is in the foyer. If travelling east, allow 30 minutes to reach Ohakune by SH 49.

Lake Taupo

Waiouru–Bulls
This section requires about two hours. Taihape is the largest centre between Taupo and Bulls, servicing both the local, rural and tourist markets. Of Taihape's cafés, Brown Sugar Café, with good coffee and year-round inviting atmosphere, is recommended by locals and travellers as the best place to fuel up and unwind.

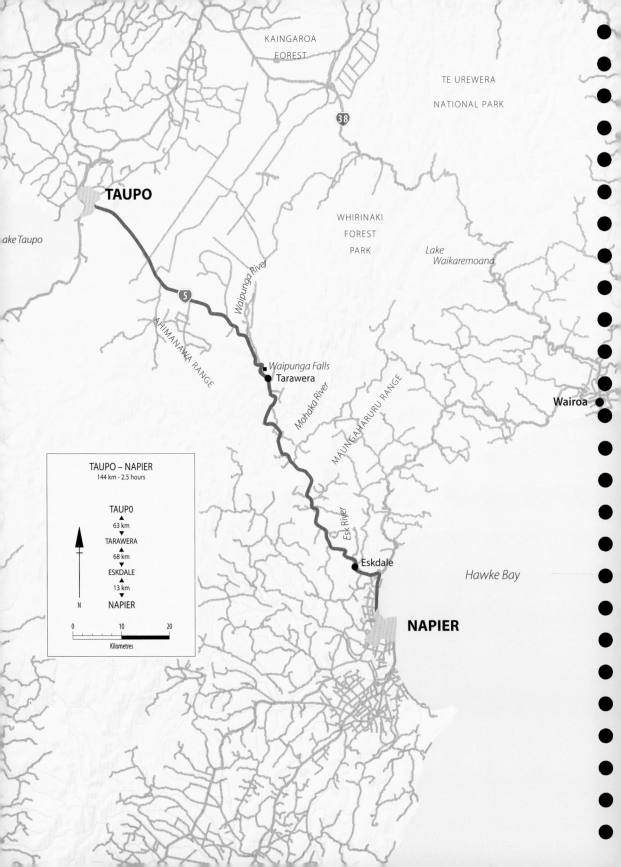

KAINGAROA
FOREST

TE UREWERA

NATIONAL PARK

38

WHIRINAKI

FOREST

PARK

Lake
Waikaremoana

TAUPO

ake Taupo

5

Waipunga River

AHIMANAWA RANGE

Waipunga Falls
Tarawera

Mohaka River

MAUNGAHARURU RANGE

Wairoa

Esk River

Eskdale

Hawke Bay

NAPIER

TAUPO – NAPIER
144 km - 2.5 hours

TAUPO
▲
63 km
▼
TARAWERA
▲
68 km
▼
ESKDALE
▲
13 km
▼
NAPIER

N

0   10   20

Kilometres

Taupo–Napier SH 5
144 km, 2 hours

Once a bush trail used by central North Island Maori and a two-day stage coach ride in colonial times, these days the Napier–Taupo highway is now entirely sealed and far from the wild ride it was even in the 1960s and 70s. The road crosses rough and remote terrain as it cuts through the Ahimanawa Range above the plantation-covered plains east of Taupo. Waipunga Falls lookout is 55 km from Taupo in the Waipunga Valley shortly before Tarawera settlement. The route then crosses the Mohaka River, climbs the Maungaharuru Range and descends to the Esk Valley wine growing area , meeting SH 2 at Bay View, 10 minutes north of Napier.

Waipunga Falls

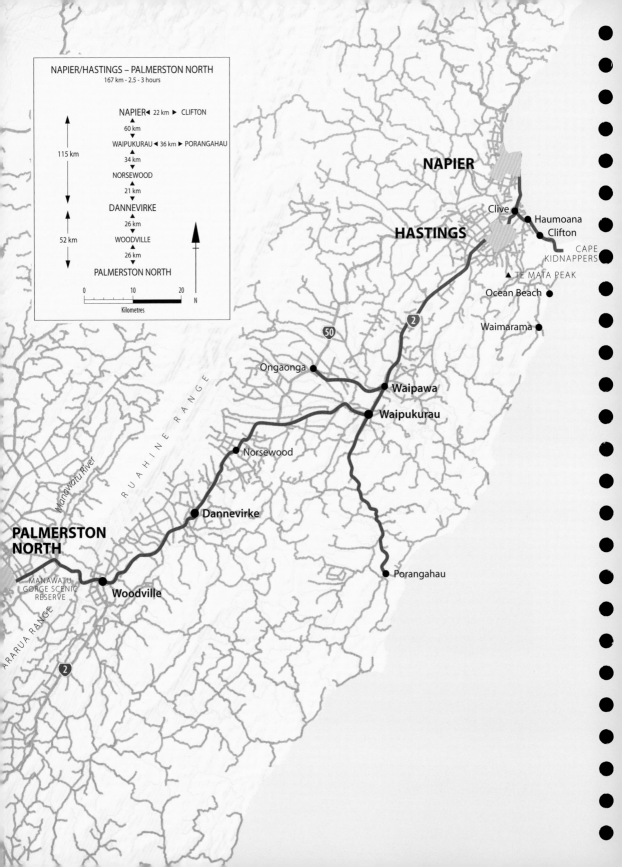

NAPIER/HASTINGS – PALMERSTON NORTH
167 km - 2.5 - 3 hours

NAPIER ◄ 22 km ► CLIFTON
▲
60 km
▼
WAIPUKURAU ◄ 36 km ► PORANGAHAU
▲
34 km
▼
NORSEWOOD
▲
21 km
▼
DANNEVIRKE
26 km
▼
WOODVILLE
26 km
▼
PALMERSTON NORTH

115 km

52 km

0   10   20
Kilometres

N

NAPIER

HASTINGS

Clive
Haumoana
Clifton
CAPE KIDNAPPERS
TE MATA PEAK
Ocean Beach
Waimarama

50

2

Ongaonga
Waipawa
Waipukurau

Norsewood

RUAHINE RANGE

Dannevirke

Manawatu River

PALMERSTON NORTH

MANAWATU GORGE SCENIC RESERVE

Woodville

Porangahau

TARARUA RANGE

2

Napier/Hastings–Palmerston North SH 2, 3
167 km, 2.5–3 hours

South of Napier and Hastings, SH 2 rolls through the dry country landscapes east of the Ruahine Range. Sheep farming is the major industry, but farm forestry, winemaking and market gardening are prominent too. Locals recommend scenic drives to Te Mata Peak, Ocean Beach and Waimarama southwest of Hastings, and to Porangahau, south of Waipukarau. The most popular diversion, however, is the trip to Cape Kidnappers.

Cape Kidnappers Gannet Reserve – campground, walks, picnicking
The Cape Kidnappers Gannet Reserve contains New Zealand's largest colony of Australasian gannets. November to late February is the best time to visit – public access is closed between July and October. To reach the colony turn off SH 2 just beyond Clive (10 km from Napier) and make for the coast at Haumoana and drive on toward Clifton (12 km). Art and craft galleries, wineries and cafés are well established between Haumoana and Clifton. The beach walk to the Cape (5 hours return) and most guided tours by vehicle begin at Scotsmans Point just short of Clifton (campground). You need to check the tides before setting out on the walk. An informative DoC brochure is available at visitor centres.

Waipawa/Waipukarau/Ongaonga
Twenty minutes from Hastings on SH 2 is the excellent Paper Mulberry Café (organic wholefoods and good coffee), while on the outskirts of Waipawa is the Abbotslee Historic Homestead and tearooms where you can enjoy fine home cooking in a gracious setting.

Waipawa and Waipukarau are bustling service towns. Waipawa's settlers museum is its main attraction, but for a real sense of the region's settler history I'd recommend the diversion west to Ongaonga (on SH 50, 17 km from Waipawa) which features numerous preserved historic buildings, 11 of which have been listed by the New Zealand Historic Places Trust. (SH 50 between Takapau and Napier is covered by a Heritage Trail brochure).

Norsewood/Dannevirke
In the hills at the base of the Ruahine Range, the tiny village of Norsewood reflects its Scandinavian heritage in its Pioneer Museum, a kids' troll trail and the country's smallest cheese factory – Rangiuru Farm – where you can sample and buy from a range of delicious organic cheeses. The Norsewear factory on Hovding St has a shop where you can buy from their famous range of woollen knitwear. In Dannevirke the hungry and thirsty can visit the State of the Art Café on the main street.

Manawatu Gorge – walks
West of Woodville, SH 3 jags toward Palmerston North through the Manawatu Gorge Scenic Reserve between the Ruahine and Tararua ranges. Two short forest walks begin at the Woodville end of the reserve.

From Palmerston North, SH 3 runs north to connect with SH 1 south of Bulls, while travelling south SH 57 connects with SH 1 near Levin. (See Bulls–Wellington, Route 30).

PALMERSTON NORTH

Woodville

Mangatainoka

Pahiatua

2

Eketahuna

Mount Bruce

LEVIN

1

Kapiti Island

TARARUA RANGE

Ruamahanga River

Waiohine River

MASTERTON

Castlepoint

Carterton

Greytown

Featherston

53

Martinborough

Lake Wairarapa

WELLINGTON

RIMUTAKA RANGE

HAURANGI FOREST PARK

Lake Ferry

Whangaimoana

Putangirua Pinnacles

Palliser Bay

TE HUMENGA PT

AORANGI RANGE

Ngawi

CAPE PALLISER

Manawatu River

RUAHINE RANGES

WOODVILLE – WELLINGTON
177 km - 3-4 hours

WOODVILLE
▲
40 km
EKETAHUNA
▲
42 km
MASTERTON ◄ 60 km ►
CASTLE POINT
37 km
82 km
FEATHERSTON ◄ 18 km ►
MARTINBOROUGH
95 km
58 km
WELLINGTON

N

0   10   20
Kilometres

Woodville–Wellington SH 2
177 km, 3–4 hours

Of the two routes to Wellington from Woodville (the other being via Palmerston North, Shannon and Levin on SH 56 or 57, 2.5 hours), this route east of the Tararua Range through Wairarapa's wide river valleys and undulating hill country offers more varied and interesting travelling.

Wairarapa's highlights include the Department of Conservation's National Wildlife Centre at Mount Bruce and rewarding drives to the coast at Castlepoint and Palliser Bay. In Southern Wairarapa craft artists, clothes designers, winemakers and restaurateurs have made the most of Wairarapa's proximity to Wellington and established a boutique shopping and café culture that has enlivened Masterton, Featherston, Greytown and Martinborough. The preservation of colonial buildings, especially in Greytown, has done much to enhance the character of these southern towns. You will find a succinct account of the region's Maori and European history in the very good *Heritage Trails of Wairarapa* booklet (free at visitor centres).

Mangatainoka/Pahiatua
Nine kilometres from Woodville, beer boffins will enjoy a tour of Mangatainoka's main attraction, the Tui Brewery. Bookings are required. Further up the Mangatainoka River is Pahiatua, a town that began as a nineteenth century roading camp in the vast totara forest that once extended between Mt Bruce and Takapau in central Hawke's Bay. 'Forty Mile Bush', as the tract between Mt Bruce and Woodville was named, was felled from the 1870s by Scandinavian immigrants contracted by the colonial government for their tree-felling and roadbuilding skills. One can only marvel at their thoroughness as you drive south through what has become prosperous sheep and dairy farming country.

Mt Bruce National Wildlife Centre – walks
The largest remnant of Forty Mile Bush occurs 17 km south of Eketahuna at Mount Bruce. Since 1962 this 945 ha reserve has been the home of the Mt Bruce National Wildlife Centre, a captive-rearing facility central to efforts to prevent the extinction of many of New Zealand's endangered birds, including takahe, kokako, stitchbird and the Campbell Island teal. Birds reared here are eventually released on offshore reserves such as Kapiti Island, or back to the wild to bolster struggling populations.

Takahe, Mt Bruce

For the public, the centre is an excellent educational facility which utilises displays, videos, and an audiovisual presentation to outline its work and the Department of Conservation's endangered species recovery programmes. Many of the endangered birds can be viewed in specially constructed forest aviaries, while brown kiwi and tuatara are housed in indoor facilities.

Easy walks through the forest of tall totara, rimu, kahikatea and tawa are likely to bring sightings of other more common forest birds. A special treat will be a sighting of North Island kaka (a large forest parrot) which have been successfully released into the forest. Kaka are fed daily at 3 p.m. as part of a supplementary feeding programme. And if you're in need of a supplementary feed yourself, there's a café at the centre.

Masterton

From Mount Bruce SH 2 crosses a spur that falls from the Tararua Range, then descends the Ruamahanga Valley to Masterton, Wairarapa's main commercial centre. Turn off at the northern end of the town for the drive to Castlepoint (see below).

Carterton/Greytown/Featherston – picnicking

Rural decline and loss of key industries has greatly affected these small rural service centres, but Greytown and Featherston have done well by refocusing on the visitor industry and heritage tourism.

The Waiohine Gorge, ten minutes north of Greytown is a popular recreational and picnicking area. Greytown residents and entrepreneurs have retained the town's colonial character by enhancing the town's classic wooden Victorian buildings, many of which now house cafés, galleries and antique shops. Papawai marae occupied an important place in New Zealand's history when it was home to the Kotahitanga (Maori Parliament) movement in the 1890s.

Featherston, at the base of the Rimutaka Range, has like Greytown retained many of its Victorian buildings, a number of which have New Zealand Historic Places Trust listings. Along with galleries and cafés, Featherston's Heritage Museum is well worth a visit.

Rimutaka Range to Wellington
1 hour

Allow an hour to reach Wellington from Featherston over the Rimutaka Range. While the highway is narrow in places there are numerous passing lanes. Snow or particularly bad weather can lead to road closures. There are toilets at the top of the range at the Pie in the Sky Café.

Featherston–Martinborough and Cape Palliser
1 hour

Martinborough

Martinborough is 15 minutes from Featherston via SH 53. Alternatively, you can bypass Featherston by taking a route direct from Greytown. Martinborough's ascent as a premiere winemaking region has boosted the town's popularity, particularly with weekend visitors from the capital. The Martinborough fairs in February and March draw tens of thousands of people. At other times of the year you can sample the region's wines, in particular its outstanding Pinot Noir, at the Martinborough Wine Centre or at boutique vineyards within walking distance from the town. Try Medici for its coffee, and the Flying Fish Café for a meal.

Palliser Bay – campground, walks, swimming, picnicking

The route to the coast at Palliser Bay begins at the Martinborough Square and skirts the Aorangi Range in Haurangi Forest Park. Shortly before Lake Ferry (motorcamp) the route turns toward Whangaimoana. The road winds for a short time above the bay offering views across Cook Strait to the South Island. When the road reaches the coast at Te Kopi look for the start of the track to the Putangirua Pinnacles (2 hours return, camping), an impressive area formed by 'badlands' erosion.

Eastern Palliser Bay has a long history of human occupation. There are burial sites all along this coast, while rock walls dating to the twelfth century at Te Humenga Pt are among the earliest evidence of Maori settlement in New Zealand. After Te Kopi the road follows the coast to Cape Palliser, much of the way being unsealed. There's a shop at the extraordinary Ngawi fishing village where the fleet is hauled ashore by tractor. Cape Palliser lighthouse is a short distance from Ngawi and the great slabs of rock called Kupe's Sails – said to be the sails that powered the canoe of Kupe, the Polynesian voyager. Seals from a nearby colony, the largest in the North Island, loll about on the rocks and in tidal pools. There are plenty of places to picnic and enjoy the coastal scenery.

Masterton–Castlepoint – campground, swimming, picnicking
1 hour
Castlepoint, another favourite Wairarapa coastal haunt, is reached via a pleasant drive through the region's eastern hill country. The route (sealed) begins at a signposted junction on the northern edge of Masterton. At Castlepoint village are spectacular cliff and headland walks, beach and safe lagoon swimming and picnicking.

Castlepoint

South Island Routes

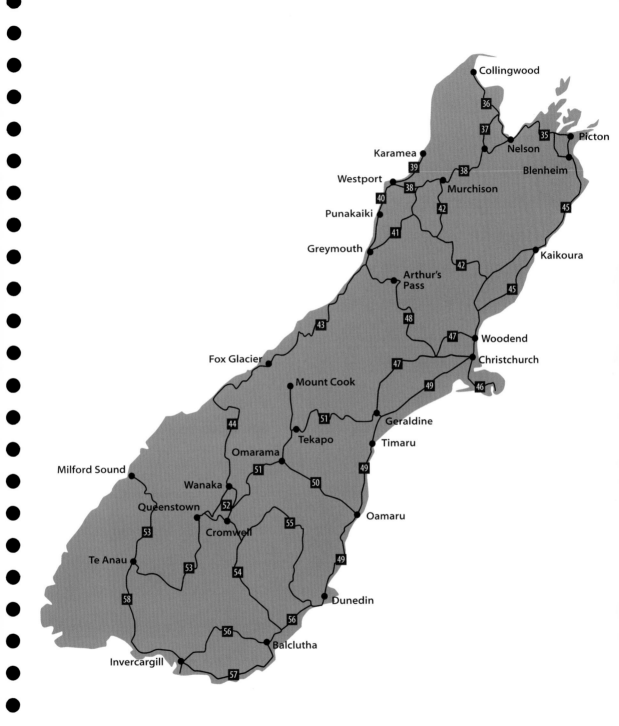

- Collingwood
- 36
- 37
- Picton
- 35
- Karamea
- Nelson
- 38
- Blenheim
- 39
- Westport
- 38
- Murchison
- 40
- 42
- 45
- Punakaiki
- 41
- Greymouth
- 42
- Arthur's Pass
- Kaikoura
- 45
- 43
- 48
- 47
- Woodend
- Fox Glacier
- 47
- Christchurch
- Mount Cook
- 49
- 46
- 51
- Geraldine
- 44
- Tekapo
- Timaru
- Omarama
- 51
- Milford Sound
- 49
- Wanaka
- 50
- Queenstown
- 52
- 53
- 55
- Oamaru
- Cromwell
- Te Anau
- 53
- 54
- 49
- 58
- Dunedin
- 56
- 56
- Balclutha
- Invercargill
- 57

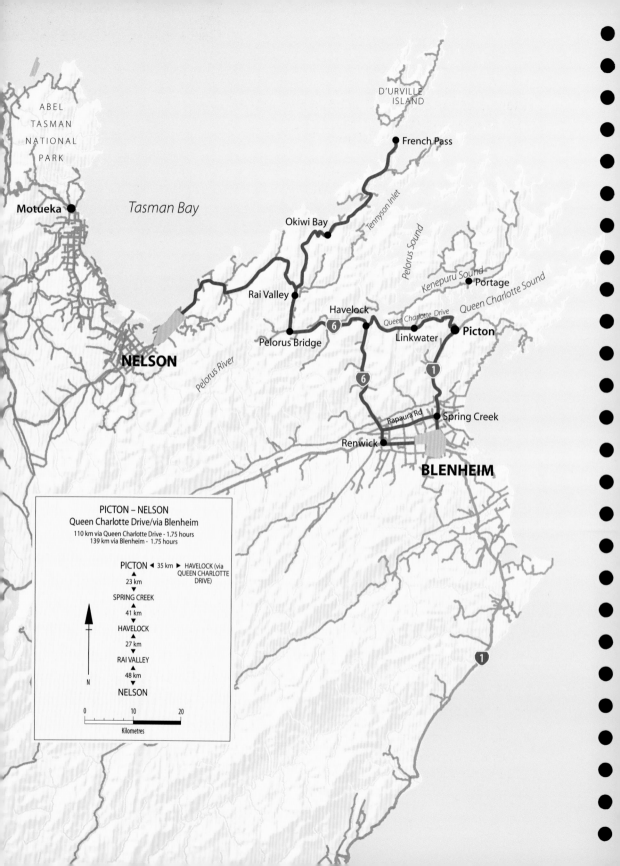

D'URVILLE
ISLAND

● French Pass

ABEL
TASMAN
NATIONAL
PARK

Tasman Bay

Motueka ●

Tennyson Inlet

Okiwi Bay ●

Pelorus Sound

Kenepuru Sound

● Portage

Rai Valley ●

Havelock
[6]

Queen Charlotte Drive

Queen Charlotte Sound

Pelorus Bridge ●

Linkwater ●

● Picton

NELSON

Pelorus River

[6]

[1]

Rapaura Rd
● Spring Creek

Renwick ●

BLENHEIM

[1]

PICTON – NELSON
Queen Charlotte Drive/via Blenheim
110 km via Queen Charlotte Drive - 1.75 hours
139 km via Blenheim - 1.75 hours

PICTON ◀ 35 km ▶ HAVELOCK (via
QUEEN CHARLOTTE
DRIVE)
▲
23 km
▼
SPRING CREEK
▲
41 km
▼
HAVELOCK
▲
27 km
▼
RAI VALLEY
▲
48 km
▼
NELSON

N

0   10   20
└──────────┴──────────┘
Kilometres

Picton–Nelson SH 6/Queen Charlotte Drive
110 km via Queen Charlotte Drive, 1.75 hours
139 km via Blenheim (Rapaura Rd), 1.75 hours

Queen Charlotte Drive is the more scenic of the routes to Nelson, however going by Rapaura Rd takes you into the heart of the Marlborough wine growing area. *The Treasured Pathway* (Nikau Press) has informed coverage of the natural and cultural heritage experienced along either of these route.

Queen Charlotte Drive – campgrounds, walks, swimming, boating
This picturesque 35 km drive links Queen Charlotte and Pelorus sounds before joining SH 6 at Havelock. Narrow and winding at times, the road has several lookouts over the sounds (Cullen Point near Havelock), and passes sublime bays with safe beaches and seaside campgrounds in Grove Arm. The Kenepuru Sound resort of Portage is 29 km (45 minutes) from Linkwater along a winding, but nonetheless scenic road. While it's possible to continue well past Portage to the outer Sounds, the roads are unsealed and drivers should seek local advice about conditions.

Nelson via Rapaura Rd (wineries)
Turning west along Rapaura Rd (leave SH 1 about 23 km south of Picton at Spring Creek) is quicker than driving into Blenheim and immediately places you in Marlborough's world famous wine-growing area. In the space of 15 km come numerous wineries – among them Hunters, Selaks, Nautilus and Babich – offering tastings, wine sales and cafés. A turn down Jacksons Rd leads to Allan Scott, Cloudy Bay and Stoneleigh wineries. SH 6 to Nelson is joined at the end of Rapaura Rd.

Havelock – campground, boating
Havelock is primarily a fishing village at the head of Pelorus Sound, but has steadily improved its offerings to travellers: try Mussel Boys restaurant for its locally grown marine produce.

Pelorus Bridge Scenic Reserve – campground, walks, picnicking, swimming
Twenty km from Havelock, this rare lowland forest remnant on the banks of the Pelorus River has been a travellers' waypoint for over 100 years. There's a great swimming hole, several short forest walks, and the café serves home-cooked food and good coffee.

From Pelorus Bridge, SH 6 passes Rai Valley, then crosses the Rai and Whangamoa saddles, a landscape dominated by the region's large pine plantations. Just past Hira, wonderful views unfold across Tasman Bay to the Abel Tasman coastline and the mountains of Kahurangi National Park.

Tennyson Inlet/French Pass
Just beyond Rai Valley a road leads off to the beautiful Tennyson Inlet (1 hour, last few kilometres unsealed from Opouri Saddle) and to French Pass (2 hours, unsealed from Okiwi Bay) in outer Pelorus Sound.

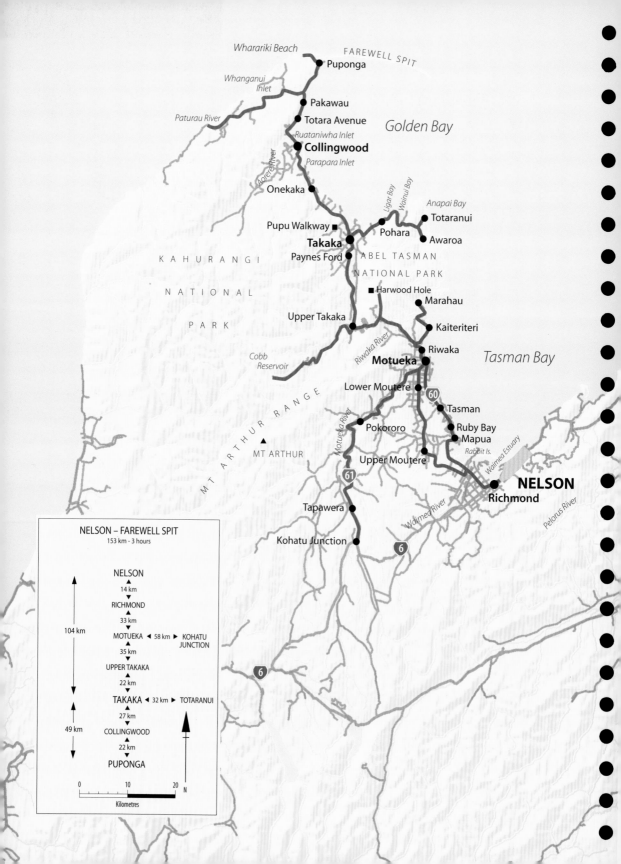

Wharariki Beach
FAREWELL SPIT
Puponga
Whanganui Inlet
Pakawau
Paturau River
Totara Avenue
Golden Bay
Ruataniwha Inlet
Collingwood
Parapara Inlet
Aorere River
Onekaka
Ligar Bay
Wainui Bay
Anapai Bay
Pupu Walkway ■
Totaranui
Pohara
Awaroa
Takaka
Paynes Ford
ABEL TASMAN
KAHURANGI
NATIONAL PARK
Harwood Hole ■
Marahau
NATIONAL
Upper Takaka
Kaiteriteri
Riwaka River
Riwaka
Tasman Bay
PARK
Motueka
Cobb Reservoir
Lower Moutere
60
Tasman
MT ARTHUR RANGE
Pokororo
Ruby Bay
Mapua
Rabbit Is.
▲ MT ARTHUR
Upper Moutere
Wairmea Estuary
61
NELSON
Motueka River
Richmond
Tapawera
Waimea River
Pelorus River
Kohatu Junction
6
6

NELSON – FAREWELL SPIT
153 km - 3 hours

NELSON
▲ 14 km
RICHMOND
▲ 33 km
104 km   MOTUEKA ◄ 58 km ► KOHATU JUNCTION
▲ 35 km
UPPER TAKAKA
▲ 22 km
TAKAKA ◄ 32 km ► TOTARANUI
▲ 27 km
49 km   COLLINGWOOD
▲ 22 km
PUPONGA

0   10   20
Kilometres

N

Nelson–Farewell Spit SH 6, 60
153 km, 3 hours

This drive combines all that makes Nelson and Golden Bay such memorable places to visit – beaches, mountain scenery and forest walks, craft galleries, wineries and cafés. Two regional guides *Art in Its Own Place* and *The Treasured Pathway* will greatly enhance the journey across the Waimea Plains, over Takaka Hill's marble landscape, and into the quieter recesses of Golden Bay. Pamphlets are available on the walks noted below.

Richmond and environs
Richmond is 14 km south of Nelson on SH 6 on the edge of Waimea Estuary and the Waimea Plains. SH 60 turns toward Motueka and Golden Bay at a roundabout south of Richmond. Between Richmond and Mapua are numerous wineries, cafés and craft galleries (all well signposted), notably Höglund's Art Glass Studio, Seifried Estate winery and Silkwood Arts and Crafts. Redwood Rd, 6 km from Richmond, leads to Rabbit Island, one of the region's best beaches.

Mapua/Ruby Bay/Tasman
SH 60 allows glimpses of Waimea Estuary as you travel toward Mapua – a pleasant seaside hamlet at the mouth of Waimea Estuary and the location of the The Smokehouse Café (formerly Mapua Nature Smoke Café) and its adjacent fish and chip shop. Ruby Bay, a kilometre up the road, has a couple of excellent winery cafés nearby, including Ruby Bay Wines. Tasman's Jester House café, with its spacious garden, playground and tame eels, has long been a family favourite, and the food's great too.

Motueka – campground
After driving around Moutere Inlet, you reach Motueka (45 minutes from Nelson) where Hot Mama's Café on the main street is still the café of choice. There's also a swimming beach and salt water baths (turn right onto Wharf Rd at the roundabout on the southern edge of the town).

Richmond–Motueka via the 'Moutere Highway'
This alternative inland route, with views of the Mt Arthur Range, is sometimes quicker than the busier SH 60. It turns off SH 60 just past the Waimea River bridge. Neudorf Vineyard is located north of Upper Moutere village, while the excellent Riverside Café is on the outskirts of Motueka at Lower Moutere.

Marahau (Abel Tasman National Park) – campground, walks, picnicking, swimming, kayaking
Beyond Motueka SH 60 crosses the Motueka River and leads toward Abel Tasman National Park and Takaka Hill. Shortly after Riwaka village, roads lead from SH 60 to Kaiteriteri Beach and to Marahau. Marahau, a 20-minute drive over the hill from SH 60, is at the southern entrance to Abel Tasman National Park and the base for sea kayaking, launch tours and walks in the park. The park's renowned beaches and coastal forests can be sampled on Tinline Walk and the return trip to Coquille Bay (both 1 hour). Don't expect solitude.

Takaka Hill – walks, views

The summit of Takaka Hill is a fascinating landscape of water-etched marble outcrops, sinkholes and caves. Though it is a slow grind to the top (prone to slips in bad weather and ice and occasional snow in winter) there are several rewarding walks and viewpoints over Tasman and Golden Bays. These include (at the base of the hill) the source of the Riwaka River; Hawke's Lookout, a short walk from SH 60 close to the summit; and the walk to Harwood Hole – a spectacular 176 m shaft – which begins 15 km down Canaan Rd (signposted) in Abel Tasman National Park. Take care on the narrow gravel road, and allow 1.5 hours for the walk. Before the road descends to the Takaka Valley is the new Takaka Hill Walkway (2–3 hours) and Harwood Lookout with outstanding views of Kahurangi National Park.

Upper Takaka/Cobb Valley – campground, walks, picnicking

A turn left at Upper Takaka leads up the Takaka River to the Cobb Power Station, and thereafter up a steep unsealed road to the Cobb Reservoir and several interesting walks. Allow 1 hour to the reservoir. The road is often narrow and winding, and not recommended for campervans.

Takaka – campground

Just before Takaka is Paynes Ford Scenic Reserve, a top rock climbing area, though it's the swimming hole here that attracts most people. Takaka (1 hour from Motueka) in high summer is the vibrant centre of Golden Bay, with its craft outlets, weekend market and eateries. The Wholemeal Café is a Takaka institution but several new places have opened in recent years – the Dangerous Kitchen and the pleasant and less threatening Milliways Restaurant among them.

Totaranui, Abel Tasman National Park

Takaka–Totaranui (Abel Tasman National Park) – campground, walks, swimming, fishing

Totaranui is 32 km (1 hour) from Takaka. The road passes Pohara Beach (campground and store) and seaside localities of Tarakohe and Ligar Bay. From Wainui Bay the road is unsealed (suitable for campervans) as it climbs over a forested range to Totaranui. Apart from the fine beach here, there is a DoC visitor centre, campground and walks toward Awaroa or Anapai bays.

Te Waikoropupu Springs/Pupu Walkway – walks

Back on SH 60, four kilometres west of Takaka, is the turnoff (at the Waitapu Bridge) to these renowned and quite beautiful springs – the clearest fresh water in the Southern Hemisphere. An easy forest walk past old gold diggings leads to the springs. The springs are sacred to Maori and swimming in them is considered a desecration of their mauri or lifeforce. The Pupu Walkway (2 hours return through mature podocarp forest) is reached via a gravelled road to the springs.

Collingwood – campground, swimming

Between Takaka and Collingwood (27 km) SH 60 stays inland until Parapara Inlet, with viewpoints over-looking Golden Bay, the Abel Tasman coastline and Farewell Spit. Expect good hospitality and food at the Mussel Inn country café and brewery at Onekaka. Collingwood, at the mouth of the Aorere River, is where you organise tours to the Farewell Spit bird sanctuary, transport to the Heaphy Track, and enjoy good food and coffee at the Courthouse Café.

Pakawau – campground

From Collingwood SH 60 skirts Ruataniwha Inlet and returns to the coast at Totara Avenue where signs warn the motorist to watch for penguins crossing the road. The road follows a long sweep of beach to Pakawau where there is a popular campground and the Schoolhouse Café. Just past Pakawau a road leads to Whanganui Inlet and Paturau River mouth on the west coast (32 km) – a five-star scenic drive, unsealed.

Puponga/Farewell Spit/Whariariki Beach – walks, picnicking

Farewell Spit Visitor Centre and Café is located a short dis-tance from Puponga on a rise overlooking the spit's high wind-whipped dunelands. Easy walking tracks lead from the centre across Puponga Farm Park to the spit's outer and inner coastlines. The (half-day) clifftop walk toward Whariariki Beach is one of the best in Golden Bay, though the shorter walk to Fossil Point is also rewarded with out-standing scenery. Much of the 24 km sandspit is an inter-nationally significant wetland for migratory wading birds and entry to all but the base of the spit is restricted. Be-tween September and March is best for observing birds.

Whariariki Beach

Ten minutes drive north of Puponga leads to a carpark and 20-minute walk across grassy dunes to the beautiful Whariariki Beach – for many the highlight of a visit to Golden Bay. You can make long walks down the beach, and watch seals in the surf off the spec-tacular Archway Islands. The track towards Farewell Spit climbs high onto cliffs and within view of seal haul-out zones and nursery areas.

Motueka–Kohatu Junction SH 61

58 km, 1 hour

A useful route to SH 6 for those travelling between Christchurch and Golden Bay. The road follows the eastern flanks of Kahurangi National Park along the Motueka River, an outstanding trout fishing river. Park access: turn off at Pokororo for the Mt Arthur road end, and at Tapawera for the Wangapeka Track. Both access roads are unsealed. Tapawera is the largest locality on SH 61, with a garage and store that serves big ice creams.

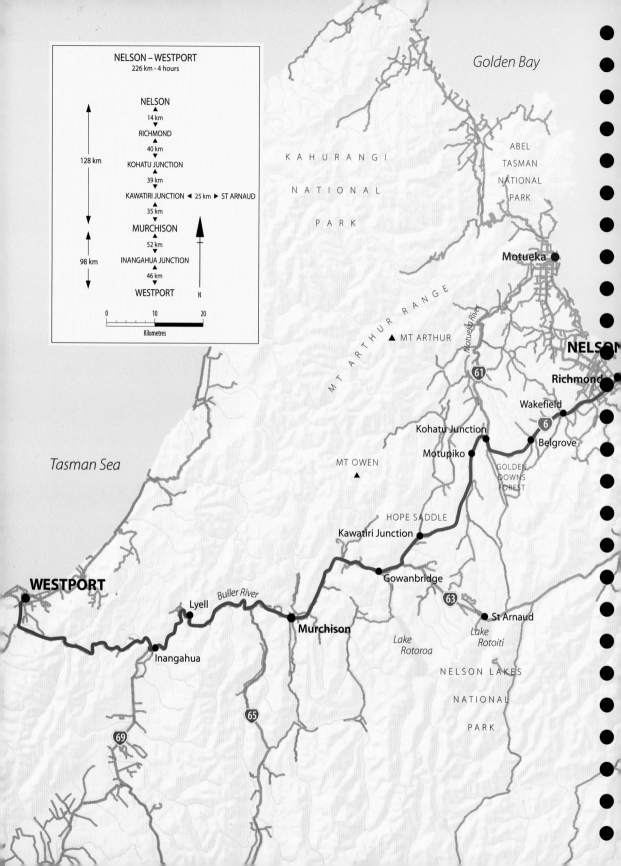

NELSON – WESTPORT
226 km - 4 hours

NELSON
▲ 14 km ▼
RICHMOND
▲ 40 km ▼
KOHATU JUNCTION
▲ 39 km ▼
KAWATIRI JUNCTION ◄ 25 km ► ST ARNAUD
▲ 35 km ▼
MURCHISON
▲ 52 km ▼
INANGAHUA JUNCTION
▲ 46 km ▼
WESTPORT

128 km
98 km

N

0   10   20
Kilometres

Golden Bay

Tasman Sea

KAHURANGI

NATIONAL

PARK

ABEL
TASMAN
NATIONAL
PARK

Motueka

M T   A R T H U R   R A N G E

▲ MT ARTHUR

Motueka River

61

NELSON

Richmond

Wakefield

6

Kohatu Junction

Belgrove

Motupiko

MT OWEN
▲

GOLDEN
DOWNS
FOREST

HOPE SADDLE

Kawatiri Junction

Gowanbridge

WESTPORT

Lyell

Buller River

63

St Arnaud

Murchison

*Lake
Rotoroa*

*Lake
Rotoiti*

Inangahua

65

NELSON LAKES

NATIONAL

PARK

69

Nelson–Westport SH 6
226 km, 4 hours

Allow a day to enjoy this drive to the West Coast. Highlights are the crossing of Hope Saddle and the journey through forested scenic reserves and earthquake-riven landscapes of the Buller Gorge. SH 6 also provides access to Nelson Lakes National Park.

Nelson–Kawatiri Junction – views, picnicking

Quick progress is made south of Nelson city past Richmond and several small rural centres to Belgrove. Past here SH 6 climbs to the crest of the Spooners Range in the heart of the vast Golden Downs pine plantation. (NB: The road that departs Belgrove through Golden Downs Forest to St Arnaud is the fastest route to Nelson Lakes from Nelson city. Allow 1.5 hours). SH 6 meets SH 61 from Motueka at Kohatu Junction (see Route 37), and thereafter continues up the Motupiko Valley toward Hope Saddle – where there are superb views of Nelson Lakes and the Kahurangi mountains. The Buller River is reached at Kawatiri Junction (picnicking and short walks). SH 63 turns here for St Arnaud (25 km) and Blenheim (127 km, 1.5 hours).

Murchison

From Kawatiri Junction the route closely follows the Buller River as it descends toward Murchison through beech forest reserves and farmed river flats. At Gowanbridge, 6 km from the junction, is the access road (sealed) to Lake Rotoroa. Near Murchison it is worth pausing for the views back toward the grey marble flanks of Mt Owen. Murchison's Rivers Café, at the Adventure Centre on Fairfax St, outshines the competition with great coffee and food.

Inangahua

Beyond Murchison the Buller enters a forested gorge with impressive rapids and huge earthquake slips. SH 6 crosses the Buller at O'Sullivans Bridge 11 km from Murchison. A few minutes further on is the somewhat contrived 'longest swingbridge in New Zealand' attraction. Save your energy for free beech forest walks at Lyell, the site of a nineteenth century mining town (camping, picnicking and historic relics). At the Inangahua Hall, residents have established a fine historic display which recounts the tremendous earthquakes that devastated the Inangahua/Murchison area in 1928 and 1967.

Buller River

Lower Buller Gorge–Westport

The slow and graceful passage of the Buller, between banks of rata forest, is a superb finale to this drive as it traces the lower gorge toward Westport.

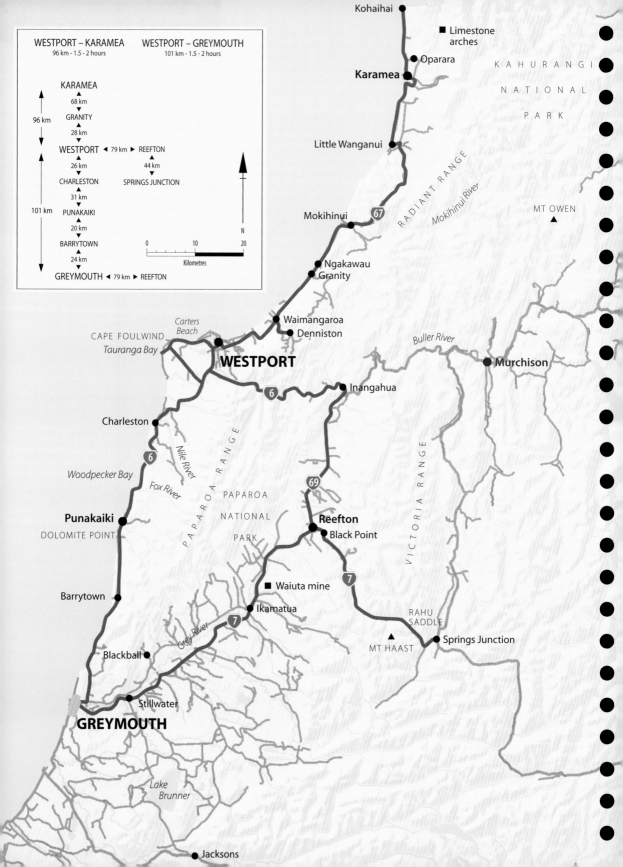

Kohaihai

■ Limestone arches

Oparara

Karamea

K A H U R A N G I

N A T I O N A L

P A R K

MT OWEN ▲

Little Wanganui

RADIANT RANGE

Mokihinui River

Mokihinui

67

Ngakawau
Granity

Buller River

Murchison

Carters Beach

Waimangaroa
Denniston

CAPE FOULWIND
Tauranga Bay

WESTPORT

6   Inangahua

Charleston

Nile River

6

Woodpecker Bay

Fox River

P A P A R O A   R A N G E

PAPAROA

NATIONAL

PARK

69

Punakaiki

DOLOMITE POINT

Reefton
Black Point

V I C T O R I A   R A N G E

■ Waiuta mine

7

Barrytown

Ikamatua

RAHU
SADDLE

7

Grey River

Blackball

MT HAAST ▲

Springs Junction

Stillwater

GREYMOUTH

Lake Brunner

Jacksons

North Westland

Westport–Karamea SH 67
96 km, 1.5–2 hours
Though it's usually less than two hours to Karamea, you can easily spend a day pottering around historic coal-mining settlements, and enjoying walks and coastal and forest scenery along the way. Terry Sumner's *Buller Walks* (Nikau Press) is an excellent guide to this area.

Denniston – views, walk
Denniston is a former coal-mining town on the Denniston Plateau, 8 km above Waimangaroa. The plateau has a stark beauty and it offers fine vistas over the coast when the weather allows. Dotted around the place are mine relics and historic buildings; the Denniston Walkway between Waimangaroa and Denniston takes 3 hours one way.

Granity/Ngakawau – walks
After a coffee at Granity's Drifters Café you can drive up the hill and walk around the old Millerton township and mine. Otherwise, three kilometres from Granity at Ngakawau is the rewarding Charming Creek Walkway which follows an old railway route through river and gorge scenery.

Mokihinui – campground
SH 67 turns inland at Mokihinui on the Mokihinui River mouth. Just over the river bridge, a left turn and short drive leads to a West Coast institution – the Cow Shed Café with its adjacent accommodation complex and coastal scenery.

Karamea Bluff Ecological Reserve
The scenic highlight of the route to Karamea is the climb up the Radiant Range through the Karamea Bluff Ecological Reserve's outstanding podocarp forest which will be ablaze with flowering rata in summer. At the base of Taffytown Hill the highway returns to coastal plains at Little Wanganui.

Karamea – campground
Karamea is the last stop before the Heaphy Track, 15 km away at Kohaihai in Kahurangi National Park. The 2 hour return walk along the Heaphy to Scotts Beach offers a taste of this beautiful forested coastline. One of New Zealand's most rewarding short walks is that to the 43 m high Oparara limestone arch in the forests of the upper Oparara Valley (turn off (signposted) 8 km from Karamea and follow the unsealed road over a steep saddle to a carpark).

Westport–Greymouth SH 6
101 km, 1.5–2 hours

The Cape Foulwind seal colony, Paparoa National Park's superb coastal scenery, and probably the only place in New Zealand where you can tuck into a buffalo meat hamburger – all within 101 km. This is another drive with enough to easily fill a day. Keep an eye out for cyclists on the narrower tracts around the coast.

Cape Foulwind seal colony – walks
The walkway to the New Zealand fur seal colony at Cape Foulwind is one of the best on the Coast. I'd recommend the 15-minute interpreted walk to the colony from the Tauranga Bay end, which is reached from Westport along SH 67a past Carters Beach and the Cape. The full walkway requires 1.5 hours one way. Back at Tauranga Bay is the superb Bay House Café. There's a direct route to SH 6 down Wilson's Lead Rd.

Charleston – campground, walks
Views of the Buckland Peaks on the northern Paparoa dominate the views inland towards Charleston, another Coast mining town well past its glory days. The short walk to the Charleston sea cliffs or along the beach from the Nile river mouth are enjoyable diversions, and you can learn much about the harshness of settler life by walking round the old Charleston cemetery above the Nile River.

Dolomite Point, Punakaiki

Fox River – walks, swimming
After Charleston the road turns inland for a stretch before returning to the coast and the languorous sweep of Woodpecker Bay, where limestone cliffs loom over the beach near the Fox River at the northern boundary of Paparoa National Park. The walk up the Fox River leads to the Fox River caves (3 hours return) and canyon (5 hours). Otherwise at low tide you can explore tidal platforms toward Seal Island.

Punakaiki – campground, walks
The drive to Punakaiki, over cliffs and headlands below spectacular limestone bluffs and coastal forest, is superb. Trumans Track, 2.5 km before Punakaiki, is a highly recommended short walk at low tide by cliffs, caves and rock pools. It's hard to avoid the crush of tourists at Punakaiki if you arrive in the middle of the day in the tourist season, but the pancake rocks and blowholes at Dolomite Point in a sou'westerly swell are always exhilarating. The best coffee and food here is at Punakaiki Crafts.

Barrytown Flats – walks, buffalos
Interspersed amongst the farmland on Barrytown Flats are remnant groves of nikau palms and lush coastal forest. At Pakiroa Beach, down the road past the Barrytown pub, fossickers occasionally turn up greenstone amongst the shingle. Of the Coast's quirky attractions, none is more so than the sight of East Asian buffalos on the hill south of the pub. No ploughs or loincloth clad farmers here – these beasts are

being fattened to be turned by the chefs at the novel Buffalo Bar and Grill into steaks, burgers and casseroles. For the buffalo-averse there's also salmon, salads, chips and other stuff.

Past Barrytown SH 6 resumes its cliff-side convolutions to Greymouth, past wind-beaten forest, glimpses up narrow canyons and hazy views over coastal headlands and the sea.

Westport–Greymouth via Reefton (Grey Valley) SH 6, 69, 7
158 km, 2.5 hours

The inland route to Greymouth traverses the eastern flanks of the Paparoa Range, down the Grey Valley from Reefton to the coast. It also connects travellers with SH 7, the quickest route between Westport and Christchurch.

The drive between Westport and Inangahua (44 km) is a wonderful drive up the lower Buller gorge with forest scenery, graceful riverbends and wide shingly rapids. At Inangahua Junction, 1 km from Inangahua, go straight ahead down the Inangahua Valley (SH 69) between the Paparoa and Victoria ranges along farmed river terraces to Reefton (34 km).

Reefton – campground, walks
Highlights of a visit here are the area's historic goldmining sites, buildings and forest walks. First stop in Reefton should be at the very good Reefton Visitor Centre on Broadway. Some of the best walks are those from SH 7 between Reefton and Springs Junction (see below). Of Reefton's cafés, Al Fresco at the eastern end of Broadway is a good choice for lunches and evening meals.

Reefton–Greymouth
79 km
From Reefton SH 7 crosses Reefton Saddle and descends to the Grey Valley's south bank. An interesting side trip is to the site of the abandoned Waiuta mine and village (signposted 23 km from Reefton, 8 km unsealed, brochure and on-site interpretation). Otherwise, you might cross the Grey at Ikamatua and drive to Blackball, visit the famous historic 'Hilton' Hotel or stock up on locally made salami. Blackball is the start of the Croesus Track across the Paparoa Range. Back on the south bank, the route to Lake Brunner and to Jacksons on SH 73 (Arthur's Pass) turns off at Stillwater.

Reefton–Springs Junction to SH 7, Lewis Pass and Christchurch
44 km, 50 minutes
The main points of interest on this lovely 50-minute drive are the craggy granite tops and beech forests of Victoria Forest Park, the Blacks Point Museum and the Murray Creek walking tracks 2 km from Reefton, the Big River Track to the Golden Lead Battery (11 km from Reefton), and the track to Mt Haast (1587 m, 6 hours return) from Rahu Saddle, one of the best walks in the area. See Murchison–Christchurch (Route 42) for the drive to Christchurch from Springs Junction.

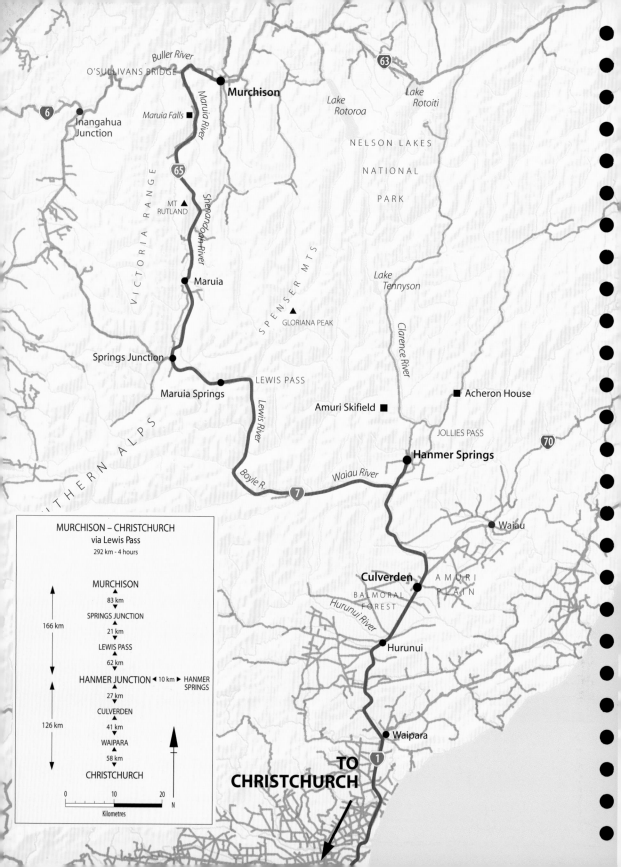

Buller River

O'SULLIVANS BRIDGE

Murchison

63

Inangahua
Junction

6

Maruia Falls

Lake
Rotoroa

Lake
Rotoiti

NELSON LAKES

Maruia River

65

MT
RUTLAND

NATIONAL

PARK

Shenandoah River

V I C T O R I A   R A N G E

S
P
E
N
S
E
R

M
T
S

Lake
Tennyson

GLORIANA PEAK

Maruia

Springs Junction

Maruia Springs

LEWIS PASS

Clarence River

Lewis River

Amuri Skifield

Acheron House

JOLLIES PASS

70

Boyle R.

7

Waiau River

Hanmer Springs

S
O
U
T
H
E
R
N

A
L
P
S

Waiau

Culverden

A M U R I
P L A I N

BALMORAL
FOREST

Hurunui River

Hurunui

Waipara

1

**TO
CHRISTCHURCH**

MURCHISON – CHRISTCHURCH
via Lewis Pass
292 km - 4 hours

MURCHISON
▲
83 km
▼
SPRINGS JUNCTION
▲
21 km
▼
LEWIS PASS
▲
62 km
▼
HANMER JUNCTION ◀ 10 km ▶ HANMER
SPRINGS
▲
27 km
▼
CULVERDEN
▲
41 km
▼
WAIPARA
▲
58 km
▼
CHRISTCHURCH

166 km

126 km

N

0   10   20
Kilometres

Murchison–Christchurch via Lewis Pass SH 65, 7, 1
292 km, 4 hours

Of the three crossings of the Alps (the others being Arthur's and Haast passes), the Lewis is easiest to drive thanks to the comparatively gentle approach up its western side. The first leg of this journey follows the Maruia Valley to its headwaters at Lewis Pass, with fine mountain scenery and corridors of upland beech in the Lewis Pass National Reserve. It then descends to the Waiau River to eventually emerge on the Amuri Plain near Culverden, and joins SH 1 at Waipara. Highlights of the drive are thermal resorts at Hanmer and Maruia Springs, forest walks in the reserve, and a rare opportunity to stand astride one of Planet Earth's continental plate boundaries.

Murchison
Murchison (see Nelson–Westport, Route 38 for more information) is on the Buller River which is followed for 11 km to O'Sullivans Bridge. Here, SH 6 to Westport crosses the bridge, and SH 65 continues ahead towards the confluence of the Buller and Maruia rivers. Between here and Springs Junction (allow an hour) the highway shadows the Victoria Range on the western side of the valley's farmed river flats, and ranges flanking the main Southern Alps chain to the east.

Maruia Falls – picnicking
This 9 m waterfall 22 km from Murchison was formed by the Murchison earthquake in 1929. Remarkably, the fall was originally about 1 m, but has grown 8 m as the riverbed below has lowered. The relatively safe runout has made running the falls popular with kayakers.

SH 65 continues up the Maruia Valley until a gorge section forces a deviation up the Shenandoah River and around Mt Rutland. The road narrows beyond Ruffe Creek and requires care in the forested gorge before the climb to Shenandoah Saddle. Beyond the saddle the route rejoins the Maruia, following wide farmed river flats to Springs Junction.

Springs Junction
SH 65 ends at Springs Junction where it meets SH 7 between Greymouth and Waipara (allow 45 minutes to cross Rahu Saddle to Reefton, see Westport–Greymouth, Route 41 for details). Despite its attractive title the Alpine Inn Café is really just a thinly disguised tearooms, but if you like white-bread sandwiches dripping with mayonnaise and everything else deep-fried, then it's the place for you.

Marble Hill Scenic Reserve – campground, picnicking
In the grassy paddock next to this innocuous little reserve, about 7 km toward Lewis Pass, the edge of the Pacific continental plate is grinding past the Indo-Australasian plate, forcing the Southern Alps skywards and skewing the West Coast northwards. Honest! This boundary, also called the Alpine Fault, runs up the western side of the Alps from Milford Sound to Nelson Lakes. Here at Marble Hill the scene of the action is a boggy terrace running across the paddock where geologists have placed a concrete wall at right angles to the fault to measure any movement. On the upper side of the terrace is the Pacific Plate, on the

lower side the Indo-Australasian. It is rare in the world to find an exact and active surface expression of a major plate boundary. It may distress some to learn that Richter 8 earthquakes along the Alpine Fault are believed to have occurred every 300 years, and one of these is well overdue. On the plus side, proximity to the fault is responsible for the thermal springs that lie ahead.

Maruia Springs – walks

From Marble Hill the road winds through beech forest next to the gravelly upper reaches of the Maruia River. About 2 km before Maruia Springs is the easy Waterfall Track (20 minutes return). The resort (98 km from Murchison) has public and private pools – the hot water is piped from the springs on the north bank of the river. The 'Hot Rocks' Café makes a passable coffee.

Maruia Springs

Lewis Pass – walks, picnicking, views

Lewis Pass is about 6 km beyond the resort after a steep climb through forest with views north toward Gloriana Peak. Just below the pass on the Canterbury side is a carpark at the start of the St James Walkway, a nice picnic spot amid alpine scenery and forests. There is a nature trail around the nearby alpine wetland, or a longer walk down to the picturesque Cannibal Gorge (2 hours return), where centuries ago Ngai Tahu warriors were said to have overwhelmed a party of Ngati Wairangi, and killed and eaten them – but don't let that put you off your lunch.

Lewis Pass–Hanmer Springs

The turnoff to Hanmer Springs is 62 km from Lewis Pass, the first 20 km of which follows the Lewis River south through corridors of beech toward the Boyle River (where the highway turns east). Now on open and scrubby farmed river terraces flanked by high ranges, the road crosses to the southern bank of the river and joins the larger braided Waiau River, generally staying high above it until the junction with SH 7a.

Hanmer Springs – campground, walks

Hanmer Springs is an alpine spa town which has been frequented by tourists since the 1860s. The main attraction, the town's outdoor thermal reserve, administered by the Department of Conservation, is a lovely place for a soothing soak. After the drought of good eateries since Murchison, Hanmer has a range of cafés and bars – for outdoor eating on a sunny afternoon the Laurel Gardens is hard to go past. There are many short walks in the Hanmer Forest, which is predominantly comprised of introduced conifers – forest trails are also popular with mountain-bikers. In winter the Amuri Skifield adds another attraction to the town's list of outdoor activities. The drive up Jollies Pass (unsealed) takes you to the edge of the high country between Hanmer and Blenheim. Acheron Accommodation House, a cob cottage built in the 1860s, now a registered historic place, is a short distance from the pass in the Clarence Valley. For several weeks during January and February each year it's possible to drive through Molesworth Station to the Awatere Valley south of Blenheim (see Picton–Christchurch, Route 45 for details). Requesting information about driving up the Clarence River to Lake Tennyson draws a guarded response from DoC: allow an hour, the road is not maintained, is very rough, and not suitable for campervans.

Culverden/Hurunui – campground

From Hanmer Springs SH 7 continues along the Waiau Valley through rolling hills to emerge on the Amuri Plain. Here the highway leaves the river and turns south toward Culverden. SH 70 to Waiau and the inland route to Kaikoura turns off just before Culverden (see Picton–Christchurch, Route 45). If you've bypassed Hanmer Springs, but are hankering for a break, try Culverden's Legacy Garden Café. Otherwise there's the historic Hurunui Hotel 13 km further past the Balmoral pine plantation (campground), just over the Hurunui River. Waipara and the SH 1 junction is 28 km away.

Highway near Springs Junction

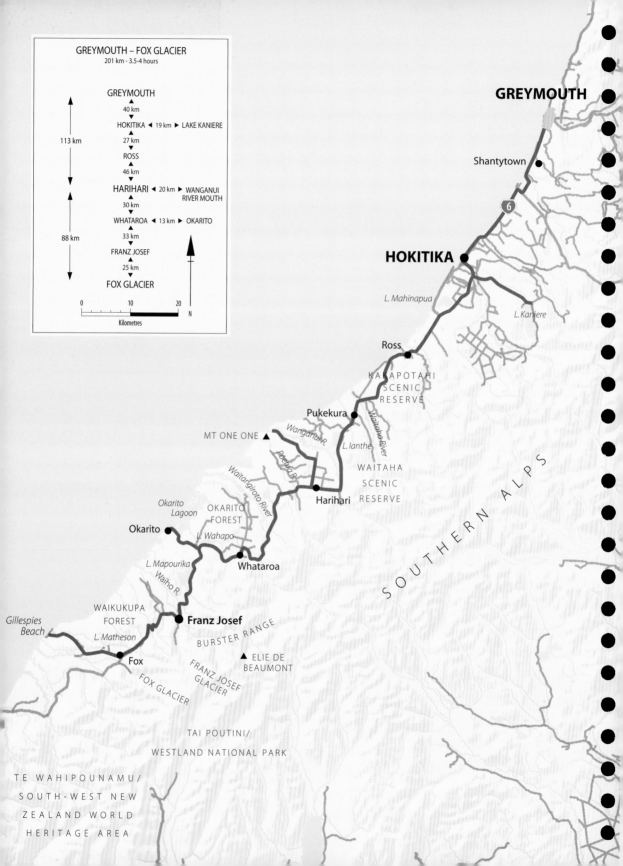

GREYMOUTH – FOX GLACIER
201 km - 3.5-4 hours

GREYMOUTH
↓ 40 km
HOKITIKA ◀ 19 km ▶ LAKE KANIERE
↓ 27 km
ROSS
↓ 46 km
HARIHARI ◀ 20 km ▶ WANGANUI RIVER MOUTH
↓ 30 km
WHATAROA ◀ 13 km ▶ OKARITO
↓ 33 km
FRANZ JOSEF
↓ 25 km
FOX GLACIER

113 km

88 km

0   10   20
Kilometres
N

GREYMOUTH

Shantytown

6

HOKITIKA

L. Mahinapua

L. Kaniere

Ross

KAKAPOTAHI SCENIC RESERVE

Pukekura

Waitaha River

Wanganui R.

MT ONE ONE ▲

L. Ianthe

WAITAHA SCENIC RESERVE

Poerua R.

Harihari

Waitangitaona River

Okarito Lagoon

OKARITO FOREST

Okarito

L. Wahapo

L. Mapourika

Whataroa

Waiho R.

WAIKUKUPA FOREST

Franz Josef

Gillespies Beach

L. Matheson

BURSTER RANGE

FRANZ JOSEF GLACIER

ELIE DE BEAUMONT ▲

Fox

FOX GLACIER

SOUTHERN ALPS

TAI POUTINI/
WESTLAND NATIONAL PARK

TE WAHIPOUNAMU/
SOUTH-WEST NEW
ZEALAND WORLD
HERITAGE AREA

Greymouth–Fox SH 6
201 km, 3.5–4 hours

Much of this memorable journey into South Westland is within sight of the high peaks of the Southern Alps. Even when it's wet (and it does rain at times!), the wild coastline, rainforests, lakes, rivers and glaciated landscapes are no less extraordinary. By the time you've gone past Whataroa you will have entered Tai Poutini/Westland National Park and the northern reaches of the vast Te Wahipounamu South-West New Zealand World Heritage Area. Some words of advice: take insect repellent and get fuel at Greymouth or Hokitika – prices at places like Whataroa and Franz Josef amount to daylight robbery.

Greymouth – campground
Greymouth, a good place to gather information about the journey south, is not short of attractions itself. They include quality coffee and home-cooked food from the Smelting House Café on MacKay St, and Shantytown, a model nineteenth century mining village 13 km south of the town. Greymouth has a number of short forest walks within the borough – covered by a DoC brochure. On dolphin-watching boat cruises, you're likely to see fur seals and coastal birds as well as the critically endangered Hector's dolphin.

Hokitika – campground, walks, picnicking, swimming, boating
Hokitika is about 30 minutes south of Greymouth and 15 minutes from the SH 73 junction (Arthur's Pass and Christchurch). The town's attractions include its jade gallery, one of the Coast's best museums, an aquarium and the William Steyn gallery. Café Flix and Café de Paris offer good food. Nineteen kilometres east of Hokitika is Lake Kaniere where an easy track along its western shores leads through the beautiful podocarp forest that lines the lake's tranquil bays. The full walk requires 4 hours one way, but shorter walks are no less rewarding. Lake Mahinapua is 10 km south of Hokitika on SH 6. There are several short walks and the 2 hour (one way) Mahinapua Walkway, but it's pleasant enough just to fetch up on the lakeshore for a picnic or to camp.

Ross – walks, picnicking
Ross is the centre of the Ross Historic Goldfields and trails like the water-race walk radiate away from the visitor centre on Aylmer St. The pride of Ross, which no-one dares criticise within earshot of the locals, is its not-so-historic opencast gold mine a few metres behind the visitor centre – the largest opencast alluvial mine in the Southern Hemisphere apparently.

Pukekura/Lake Ianthe – campground, picnicking
South of Ross, the highway traverses corridors of rimu and matai forest in the Kakapotahi and Waitaha Scenic Reserves. Up the hill from the Waitaha River at Pukekura is the Lake Ianthe Tavern, and over the road the quaint 'Bushman's Centre' dedicated to the bushman's arts. The café is unexceptional. Lake Ianthe is a large forest-fringed glacial lake, popular with swimmers, campers and anglers.

Harihari – campground, walks, picnicking

From Lake Ianthe SH 6 turns inland toward the foothills of the Southern Alps. The 20 km side trip from Harihari to the Wanganui River mouth leads to one of the lesser-known gems on the coast – the 45-minute walk to the Mt One One (Doughboy) lookout where superb views unfold across unbroken forest to the Alps. You can continue along the coast on the Harihari Coastal Walk to the Poerua River mouth. The Mt One One–Poerua circuit (3 hours) is described in a brochure available at Harihari.

Whataroa

Tours of the white heron colony at Waitangiroto Lagoon are the major attraction at Whataroa. The prominent peak seen from several places between Whataroa and Franz Josef is Elie de Beaumont (3109 m).

Southern Alps from Lake Mapourika

Okarito Lagoon – walks, picnicking

A couple of kilometres past Lake Wahapo is the 13 km road to Okarito, a small community of baches and homes on a magnificent stretch of coast bordering Tai Poutini/Westland National Park. Okarito's rimu forests are a symbol of the successful battle against loggers in the 1980s – their addition to the national park has protected intact a sequence of ecosystems from coast to mountains – rare not just in New Zealand but in the world. Since then it's been learned that the Okarito brown kiwi is a distinct sub-species – recent government funding has established a kiwi sanctuary here. On a fine day the view from Okarito Trig (1.5 hours return) across Okarito Forest to the high peaks of the national park is incomparable. Bird-watching by hired canoe on Okarito Lagoon and beach walks are other popular activities.

Lake Mapourika – campground, fishing, picnicking, boating, swimming

Lake Mapourika, 11 km from Franz Josef is the largest and most scenic of South Westland's glacial lakes. Like the much larger 'great lakes' east of the Alps, these lakes were created as glaciers retreated when the last Ice Age waned 10,000–13,000 years ago.

Franz Josef – campground, walks

Franz Josef Glacier has been a tourist icon since the late nineteenth century, and they come still in ever increasing numbers to see it. Take your hat, coat and sensible shoes (and earplugs if you're averse to aircraft noise) for the walk to the base of the glacier (1.5 hours return) which begins up the Waiho Valley. Be especially careful not to get close to the unstable terminal face of the glacier. A roadend kiosk within sight of the glacier has an informative series of interpretive panels on glacier formation and the story of the Franz. Guided walks onto the glacier can be arranged at the village. Other high quality shorter walks in the valley include those to Peters Pool, Lake Wombat and to Sentinel Rock – the latter offering good

Sheep grazing near Fox Glacier with Mt Tasman and Aoraki/Mt Cook behind

views of the glacier. A more demanding but high reward trip is the day walk to Alex Knob on the Burster Range with panoramic views of the glacier's upper névés and peaks, and the coast. Information on these walks can be gleaned from the DoC visitor centre at the Tai Poutini/Westland National Park headquarters.

Fox – campground, walks

The 25-minute drive to Fox covers steep forested terrain as it crosses Cook Saddle. Fox village isn't as developed as Franz Josef, though even that status is changing rapidly. For walkers, access to the glacier is easier and quicker (1 hour return) than the Franz, and it benefits too from the long established company Alpine Guides Westland whose guides and guided walks enjoy a good reputation. The Fox Glacier terminal is no less dangerous than the Franz. Fox's most regarded walk is the easy circuit through the forests around Lake Matheson (reached off Cook Flat Rd toward the coast), famous for its reflections of the Southern Alps at dawn and dusk. When evening light colours the mountains, Gillespies Beach, 19 km from Fox through Waikukupa Forest (unsealed), is a wonderful place to be.

Walkers on the terminal of the Fox Glacier

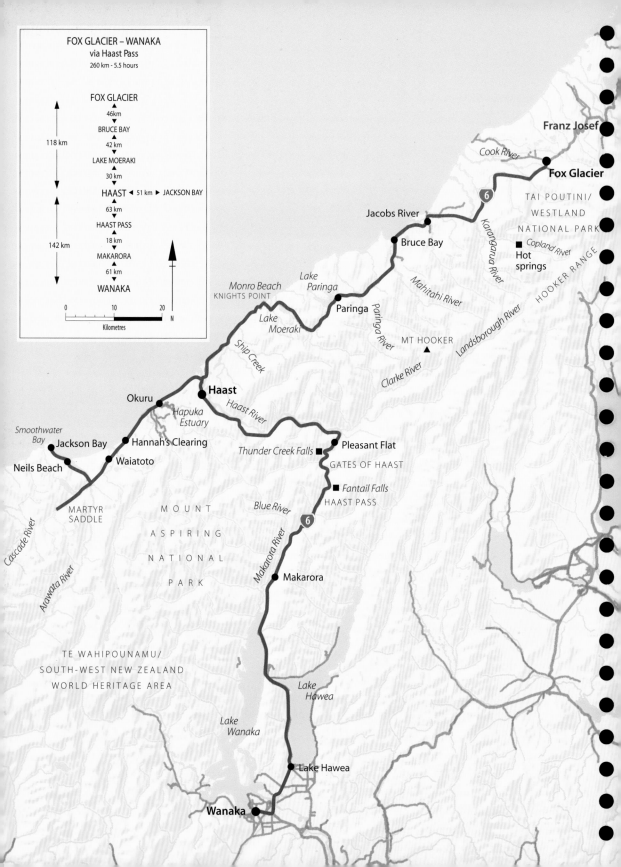

FOX GLACIER – WANAKA
via Haast Pass
260 km - 5.5 hours

FOX GLACIER
▲
46km
BRUCE BAY
▲
42km
LAKE MOERAKI
▲
30km
HAAST ◄ 51 km ► JACKSON BAY
▲
63km
HAAST PASS
▲
18km
MAKARORA
▲
61km
WANAKA

118 km

142 km

0   10   20
Kilometres

N

Franz Josef

Cook River

Fox Glacier

6

TAI POUTINI/
WESTLAND
NATIONAL PARK

■ *Copland River*
Hot
springs

Jacobs River

Karangarua River

Bruce Bay

HOOKER RANGE

Mahitahi River

Lake
Paringa

Monro Beach
KNIGHTS POINT

Paringa

Paringa River

MT HOOKER ▲

Landsborough River

Lake
Moeraki

Ship Creek

Clarke River

Haast

Haast River

Okuru

Hapuka
Estuary

Smoothwater
Bay

Jackson Bay   Hannah's Clearing

Thunder Creek Falls ■   Pleasant Flat

Neils Beach   Waiatoto

GATES OF HAAST

■ *Fantail Falls*
HAAST PASS

MARTYR
SADDLE

M O U N T

Blue River

6

Cascade River

A S P I R I N G

Makarora River

Arawata River

N A T I O N A L

Makarora

P A R K

Lake
Hawea

TE WAHIPOUNAMU/
SOUTH-WEST NEW ZEALAND
WORLD HERITAGE AREA

Lake
Wanaka

Lake Hawea

Wanaka

Fox Glacier–Wanaka via Haast Pass SH 6
260 km, 5.5 hours

The drive between Fox Glacier and Wanaka is dominated by the coastal, forest and mountain landscapes that form the central portion of the Te Wahipounamu South-West New Zealand World Heritage Area. From Haast, the road jags inland for the crossing of Haast Pass to Otago's gentler, beech-forested landscape and the shores of Lake Wanaka. Highlights of the route are the many short walks to a variety of coastal and forest features, perfect for the traveller. Although described as a southward journey below, the best experience of it in my opinion is travelling northwards from Wanaka, leaving around 2 p.m. and driving as the late afternoon and evening sun lights the high peaks and forests between Haast and Fox.

Fox Glacier–Bruce Bay – walks, picnicking
The 46 km drive to Bruce Bay crosses the coastal plains formed by the Cook and Karangarua rivers. Single lane suspension bridges carry you across these two large fast-flowing rivers – the latter, 30 minutes from Fox, provides access to the Copland Track to Welcome Flat Hut and its nearby hot springs (6–8 hours one way). There's a dangerous accident black spot where the highway crosses Jacobs River. Bruce Bay, littered with driftwood and lined to the north by rimu forest and ranks of flax, marks a brief return to the coast before the highway again enters forests up the Mahitahi River. Views inland from here reach toward remote peaks and snowfields of the Hooker-Landsborough Wilderness Area.

Paringa – campground, picnicking
The route between Bruce Bay and Lake Moeraki stays inland, wending through tall dark South Westland forests much of the way. At the Paringa River the route opens briefly onto river plains. On the northern bank is the Salmon Farm Café, a pleasant spot for a break where farmed salmon swim aimlessly in their tanks, and fat trout lurk in the adjacent stream. Lake Paringa is enclosed by forest and is a popular swimming, camping and picnicking area.

Lake Moeraki/Monro Beach – walks, picnicking
Just past Lake Moeraki and close to the Lake Moeraki Wilderness Lodge is the forest track to Monro Beach and the Whakapohai Wildlife Refuge (40 minutes one way). The refuge protects breeding areas used by tawaki (Fiordland crested penguin) between July and December.

Knights Point lookout/ Ship Creek – views, picnicking, walks
Four kilometres past Lake Moeraki SH 6 reaches the spectacular coastline north of Haast at Knights Point. After winding around steep headlands and gullies, the road returns to forested coastal plains and a series of dune ridges. At Ship Creek is an excellent 20-minute kahikatea swamp forest walk – primeval scenery which has made photographers and film-makers wealthy

Bruce Bay

and is the delight of ecologists who regard these area's forests as the best representation anywhere of Mesozoic-era swamp forests that existed 100 million years ago. Ship Creek's 30-minute Dune Lake circuit through wind-stunted forest offers fine views over lake and coastline.

Haast

Haast is heralded by the crossing of the wide and braided Haast River. Inside the gleaming corrugated-iron Haast Visitor Centre is information on the World Heritage Area and brochures on the walks noted in this section. Haast is the last place for fuel until Makarora (81 km) on the Otago side of Haast Pass. See below for the Haast–Jacksons Bay description.

Haast River

The way to Haast Pass follows the Haast River to its headwaters, probably the most dramatic of any of the road crossings of the Alps. SH 6 traces the south bank of the river beneath alpine tops and steep forested valley walls on the boundary of Mount Aspiring National Park. Where the Landsborough River joins the Haast, about 40 km from the coast, the Haast River and SH 6 make an abrupt turn south.

Pleasant Flat – campground, picnicking

Located a few kilometres from the Haast-Landsborough confluence, on a fine day Pleasant Flat is indeed pleasant. Vistas spread north up the Landsborough and Clarke valleys to the impressive southern face of Mt Hooker and peaks of the Hooker Range – the centrepiece of the Hooker/Landsborough Wilderness Area.

Gates of Haast – views, walks

Next to the flat, the highway crosses the Haast River and enters the Mount Aspiring National Park and the breathtaking Gates of Haast, a narrow and dramatic gorge where slips and enormous boulders choke the river's passage. It is hard to imagine that the easy flowing river a few kilometres on is the source of this imbroglio which cuts steeply down toward the coast. After a second crossing of the river are two short and rewarding forest walks to Thunder Creek and Fantail falls.

Haast Pass (563 m)

West of the pass the forests are dominated by kamahi, but on the pass itself, atop a gentle rise above the headwaters of the Haast River, silver beech is the most common tree. The Haast is the lowest of the three Southern Alps passes, and, as an interpretive panel notes, it was a well-known route used by Maori. The pass was first reached by a European explorer, J.H. Baker, in 1861 but was then controversially named after Julius von Haast who crossed it to the West Coast in 1863. A packhorse trail over the pass was established by the 1870s, but construction of the highway between Hawea and Haast was spread across no less than 36 years between 1929 and 1965!

Haast Pass–Makarora – campground, walks, picnicking

From the pass you are soon into gentler topography at the head of the Makarora Valley. Towards Lake Wanaka the highway follows the bed of the steadily broadening valley which was formed by one of many gargantuan glaciers that flowed through the area during the Pleistocene Ice Age. There are camping/picnic sites and walks at Cameron and Davis flats, and a 30-minute walk to beautiful river pools at the mouth of the Blue River. At Makarora there is a DoC visitor centre, campground, store and tearooms.

Lakes Wanaka & Hawea

Most of the 61 km drive between Makarora and Wanaka is high above these impressive glacier-formed lakes. There are a number of lookouts and picnicking sites where you can enjoy lake and mountain scenery, including the camping area at Boundary Creek. See Christchurch–Wanaka (Route 51) for information about services at Wanaka.

Haast–Jackson Bay
51 km, 45 minutes

The short stretch of highway to Jackson Bay, along the coastal strip west of Mount Aspiring National Park, leads to remote beaches and rivers as well as forest and mountain scenery and several interesting walks.

Hapuka Estuary Walk – walk

Just past Okuru is this easy 20-minute walk through coastal forest and the Hapuka Estuary intertidal zone. It is one of those rare places (in the world) where wetlands are given due for the important ecological role they play. Forest and coastal birds are likely to be seen, while information panels provide natural history interpretation.

Rainforest, South Westland

Jackson Bay – walks

From Hannah's Clearing the road enters a beautiful corridor of forest, emerging briefly where it crosses the Waiatoto. At the legendary Arawata River the sealed route turns west to Neils Beach where a bumpy sandy road leads to the Arawata mouth, and a wild beach – watch for penguins! At Jackson Bay a DoC shelter and information kiosk opposite the wharf describes both the natural and cultural history of the Bay, and you can enjoy takeaways at The Craypot. Walks from here lead to Wharekai Te Kau wildlife refuge (20 minutes, information panels) and Smoothwater Bay (3–4 hours return).

Red Hills Lookout – views

A 22 km unsealed route from just past the Arawata River bridge leads to a lookout over the Cascade River and rugged surrounding hinterland. A lookout (with natural history information panels) 3 km past Martyr Saddle offers views south over the valley toward the Red Hills – a region of outstanding natural and wilderness values.

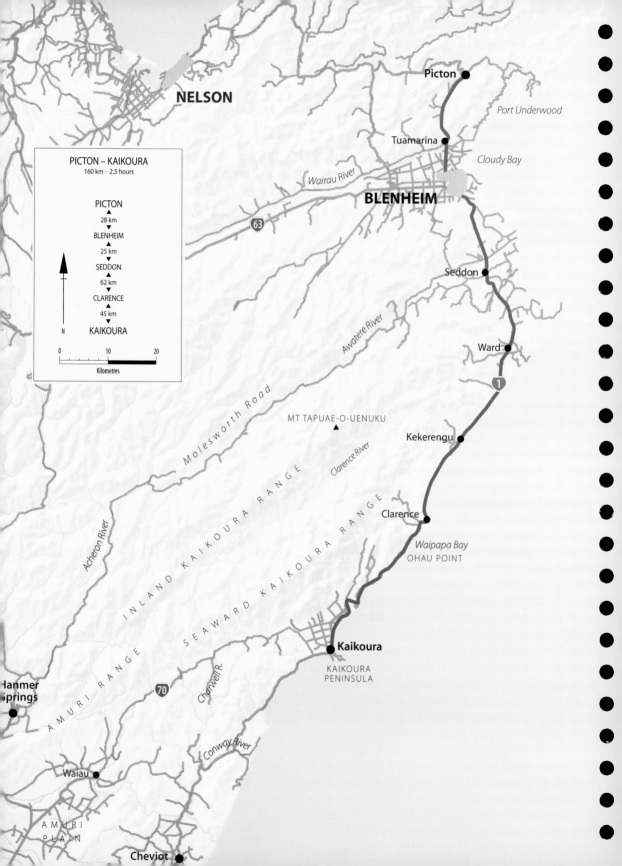

NELSON

Picton

Port Underwood

Tuamarina

Cloudy Bay

Wairau River

63

BLENHEIM

Seddon

Awatere River

Ward

1

MT TAPUAE-O-UENUKU

Kekerengu

Clarence River

Clarence

Waipapa Bay
OHAU POINT

Molesworth Road

INLAND KAIKOURA RANGE

SEAWARD KAIKOURA RANGE

Acheron River

Kaikoura

KAIKOURA
PENINSULA

Hanmer
Springs

70

Charwell R.

AMURI RANGE

Conway River

Waiau

AMURI
PLAIN

Cheviot

PICTON – KAIKOURA
160 km - 2.5 hours

PICTON
▲
28 km
▼
BLENHEIM
▲
25 km
▼
SEDDON
▲
62 km
▼
CLARENCE
▲
45 km
▼
KAIKOURA

N

0   10   20
Kilometres

Picton–Christchurch SH 1

346 km, 5 hours

SH 1 is the busy main route south to Christchurch. Beginning in Marlborough's world class wine-growing region, SH 1 passes to Kaikoura's famed whale, dolphin and seal-watching coast before crossing to the Canterbury Plains.

Picton –Kaikoura, 160 km, 2.5 hours

Picton – campground

The Picton Visitor Centre, on the waterfront a few hundred metres from the ferry terminal, is a useful place to collect information on the places ahead. One of these occurs after 19 km at Tuamarina on the edge of the Wairau Valley – the site of the Wairau massacre (1843), a disgraceful incident where Maori defending their land rights were gunned down by colonists.

Blenheim – campground

Blenheim was one of New Zealand's earliest settlements, its current prosperity founded on the region's suitability for sheep farming and horticulture. These days its fame as a winegrowing region has encouraged an attractive café, wine and craft-trail culture (see also Picton–Nelson, Route 35) that draws people from all over the globe.

Seddon/Ward – campground, views

Just south of Blenheim is the large Montana winery, after which SH 1 crosses Dashwood Pass to Seddon in the Awatere Valley. From here the vistas west are filled by the foothills rising toward Mt Tapuae-o-Uenuku (2885 m) and its outriders on the Inland Kaikoura Range. (See also the Molesworth Road description below).

Kekerengu & Kaikoura Coast – campground

The first leg of the Kaikoura coast highway to Clarence River lies between steep hillsides and a 30 km shingle beach. Halfway down the beach at Kekerengu is 'The Store' (named after its humble predecessor), a fine café, craft shop and gardens. Best of all is the uninterrupted sea view from the porch while you're enjoying coffee and cake.

At the Clarence River you're confronted by the eastern wall of the Seaward Kaikoura Range, which rises an incredible 2500 m in just 12 km from the sea – a faster rise than most of the Southern Alps. Further inland are the southeastern faces of the Inland Kaikoura peaks. Freshly cooked crayfish are sold from roadside caravans on the rocky coast at the base of the range. There's a DoC campground at Waipapa Bay, and a lookout over the Ohau Point seal colony which is well worth stopping to view.

Kaikoura – campground, walks, marine mammal watching

Kai means food, koura means crayfish, however it's watching ocean mammals that has transformed Kaikoura from crayfishing port to tourist mecca in the last decade. Once you've recovered your land legs, and enjoyed lunch at one of Kaikoura's many cafés, make the circuit or a shorter walk on Kaikoura Penin-sula with its seal colonies, birdlife, and great views of the Kaikoura mountains and coast. DoC has done a good job with the displays and information on Kaikoura's natural and human history at the town's visitor centre on the waterfront.

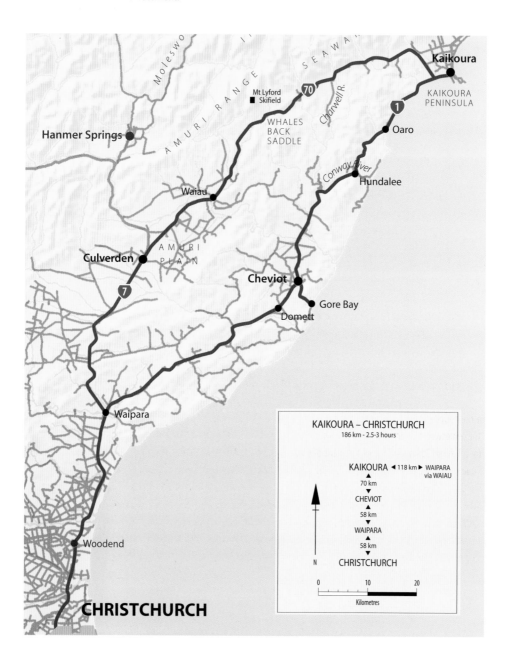

KAIKOURA – CHRISTCHURCH
186 km - 2.5-3 hours

KAIKOURA ◀118 km▶ WAIPARA
via WAIAU
▲
70 km
▼
CHEVIOT
58 km
▼
WAIPARA
58 km
▼
N   CHRISTCHURCH

0   10   20
Kilometres

Kaikoura–Waipara via Waiau SH 70, 7
118 km, 2 hours

This is a scenic alternate route to Waipara with fine views of the Seaward Kaikoura and Amuri ranges and distant Mt Tapuae-o-Uenuku. SH 70 strikes inland 4 km south of Kaikoura, and contrary to current maps the road is now entirely sealed. The turnoff to Mt Lyford skifield is reached after the road crosses Whales Back Saddle from the Charwell Valley.

 Waiau is a sleepy village with a store, garage and a couple of pubs. The Ramshead Café and Bar (more bar than café) makes nice scones but head for Hanmer or to Culverden's Legacy Gardens Café for a break. SH 7 is 19 km from Waiau, and Hanmer Springs 52 km.

Kaikoura–Waipara SH 1
70 km, 1 hour

 Cheviot – picnicking
South of Kaikoura at Oaro the road climbs through the rural hill country as it crosses the Hundalee Hills to the Conway River. Gore Bay, 15 minutes east of Cheviot, is a popular surf beach with safe swimming, picnic sites and a campground. There's no shop. Cheviot has a couple of tearooms, but the best food and coffee hereabouts is 6 km further south at Domett's Mainline Station café – a converted railway station.

 Waipara
SH 1 descends to the Canterbury Plains down the Greta Valley. Waipara is at the junction with SH 7 from Lewis Pass and Hanmer Springs. Several wineries have opened cafés here, while every Sunday from January to the end of March the Weka Pass steam train excursion departs at 11.30 a.m. and 2 p.m. (for the remainder of the year the train runs on the first and third Sundays of the month).

Allow 45 minutes to an hour to reach central Christchurch from Waipara. Those travelling to Arthur's Pass can turn off at Woodend and travel via Oxford to reach SH 73 at Waddington (58 km). (See Woodend–Geraldine, Route 47).

Molesworth Road
The Molesworth Road between the Awatere Valley (south of Blenheim) and Hanmer Springs is opened each summer for a limited season by the Department of Conservation, usually between New Year and early February. Molesworth Road crosses historic Molesworth Station, a large inland Marlborough sheep and cattle run; the area's dry-country landscapes are often stunning, especially in the upper Awatere Valley as it rounds the Inland Kaikoura Range, and in the Acheron Valley. Between the upper Awatere and Hanmer Springs the road is unsealed but usually passable to all vehicles. There are no facilities and travellers are advised to be well-prepared for breakdowns, flat tyres etc. There is a fee to use the road. Camping is possible at each end, but not within the station itself. When the fire risk is high, the road will be closed. A brochures about the route is available from visitor centres.

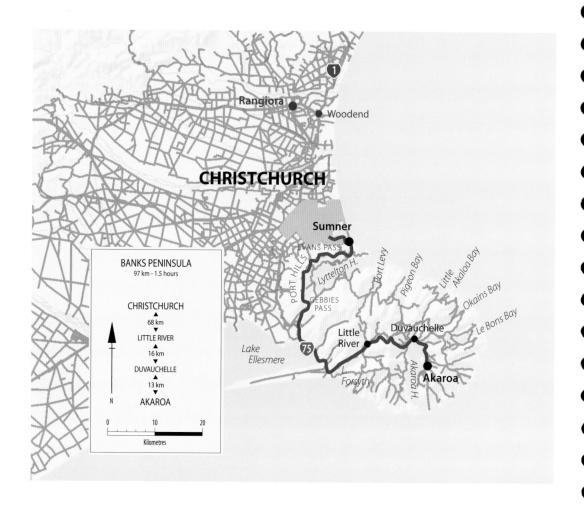

Banks Peninsula
Christchurch–Akaroa via Port Hills & SH 75
97 km, 1.5 hours

This rewarding scenic route to Akaroa on Banks Peninsula begins on the Summit Road on Christchurch's Port Hills. The return journey can be made via the peninsula's remote harbours and bays on its northern coastline – in total an enjoyable day excursion from Christchurch.

Summit Road
Drive to Sumner village and take the road to Evans Pass. A right turn at the pass puts you on the Summit Road, which follows the crest of the Port Hills to Gebbies Pass (1 hour). Exceptional views across Lyttelton Harbour and the Canterbury Plains can be experienced from a number of walks and viewpoints en route. The road is narrow and must be shared with cyclists, runners and walkers.

Little River

Below Gebbies Pass, SH 75 is joined at the Black Tulip Store (petrol). The road now skirts the shallow Lake Ellesmere and turns northeast towards Lake Forsyth and Little River village. Little River Café offers great coffee and lunches.

Barrys Bay/Duvauchelle – campground, swimming, fishing

From Little River the road climbs to a saddle below French Hill with views over Akaroa Harbour from the Hilltop Tavern. Cabbage trees line the harbour at Barrys Bay where you can buy locally made cheeses or drive 3 km around the west side of the harbour to French Farm winery. The Hotel des Pecheurs at Duvauchelle is the first intimation of the Peninsula's Gallic influence. Just down the road the French ensign flies over the old Post and Telegraph office, now a stylish café with views down the harbour.

Akaroa – campground, swimming, fishing

Historic homes nestle amid the new at Akaroa which markets its French heritage to the hilt. European architecture, cafés, wine bars, galleries and craft shops lend a relaxed Mediterranean air to the settlement. Among the range of adventure activities that can be purchased is the opportunity to see the rare Hector's dolphin with the Godley Head Dolphin Company.

A recommended return journey to Christchurch is along the summit road above Akaroa back to the saddle at the Hilltop Tavern. From Akaroa take Long Bay Rd (past Akaroa Winery and Café) and turn left onto the summit road. As well as offering fine views, the road provides access to Le Bons, Okains, Little Akaloa and Pigeon bays. There's a serviced motor camp at Le Bons Bay, and a museum, shop and fuel at Okains. The unsealed route between Pigeon Bay and Port Levy is suitable for four-wheel drive vehicles only.

Banks Peninsula

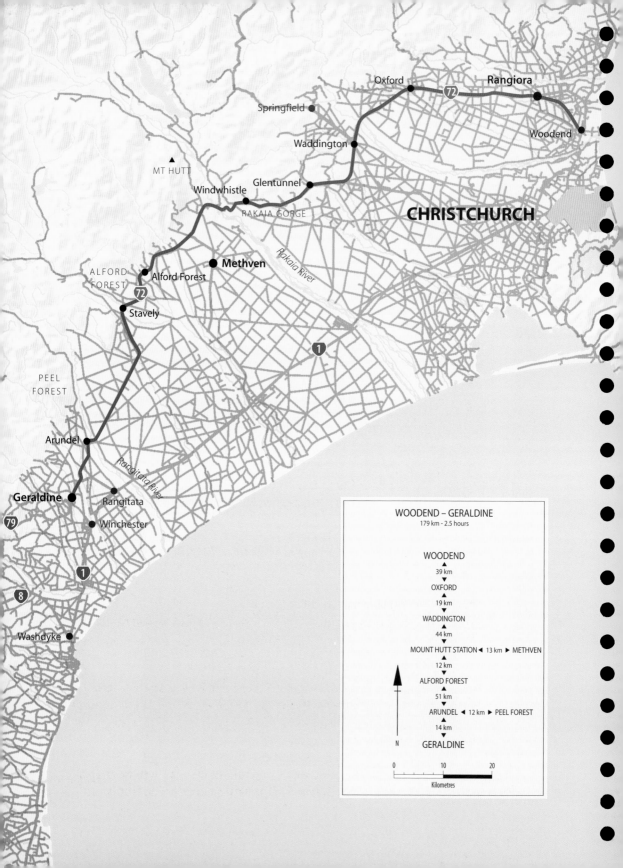

Oxford

Rangiora

72

Springfield

Woodend

Waddington

MT HUTT

Glentunnel

Windwhistle

RAKAIA GORGE

CHRISTCHURCH

Rakaia River

Methven

ALFORD FOREST

Alford Forest

72

Stavely

1

PEEL FOREST

Arundel

Rangitata River

Geraldine

Rangitata

79

Winchester

1

8

Washdyke

WOODEND – GERALDINE
179 km - 2.5 hours

WOODEND
▲
39 km
▼
OXFORD
▲
19 km
▼
WADDINGTON
▲
44 km
▼
MOUNT HUTT STATION ◄ 13 km ► METHVEN
▲
12 km
▼
ALFORD FOREST
▲
51 km
▼
ARUNDEL ◄ 12 km ► PEEL FOREST
▲
14 km
▼
GERALDINE

N

0   10   20
Kilometres

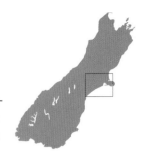

Woodend–Geraldine SH 72
179 km, 2.5 hours

SH 72, the 'Inland Scenic Route', bypasses Christchurch by tracing the western edge of the Canterbury Plains. It's also a convenient bypass to SH 73 (Arthur's Pass) for those travelling from Picton, and a less busy route to Mount Cook. Highlights are the Rakaia Gorge, Mt Hutt and the Peel and Alford forests.

Woodend–SH 73 Junction at Waddington
Like much of this route, the 30-minute drive to Waddington via Rangiora and Oxford townships traverses the flat expanses of the Canterbury Plains. At the SH 73 junction at Waddington, turn east down SH 73 for about 1 km to return to the Inland Scenic Route.

Rakaia Gorge – campground, walks, fishing
The countryside hereabouts is a mix of sheep farms, forests and market gardens set against the backdrop of rising hills towards Mt Hutt. Glentunnel and Windwhistle are quiet country localities each with a store and a garage. Not far from Windwhistle the route drops sharply into the Rakaia Valley just below the Rakaia Gorge. Jetboating and salmon fishing on this large glacial river are popular activities, as is walking the gorge walkway (3–4 hours return). The Homestead at Mt Hutt Station, on the southern terrace above the river, serves teas, coffees and lunches.

Mt Hutt/Methven – skiing
The turnoff to Mt Hutt Skifield is 7 km from Mt Hutt Station (the skifield road is closed in summer). Methven, a 13 km detour off SH 72, has a good information centre, and a number of cafés. Try Café 131.

Alford Forest – walks, picnicking
Alford Forest about 4 km northwest of Stavely has a number of walks including the excellent Sub-alpine Walkway.

Peel Forest – campground, walks, picnicking, fishing
This 550 ha native forest reserve close to the Rangitata River is a popular holiday location 12 km north of Arundel.

Geraldine – campground
A pleasant mid-Canterbury town, and a waypoint for those travelling to Mount Cook or further south. I can recommend the delights of the Berry Barn bakery on the main street (but avoid arriving the same time as a busload of tourists), while the nearby Easy Way Café makes a passable coffee and good lunches. Some will also enjoy the town's vintage car museum.

From Geraldine, drive south 11 km to Winchester to rejoin SH 1. If travelling to Mount Cook and the Mackenzie Country, take SH 79 to Fairlie (46 km, 45 minutes) and join SH 8 from Washdyke (see Christchurch–Wanaka, Route 51).

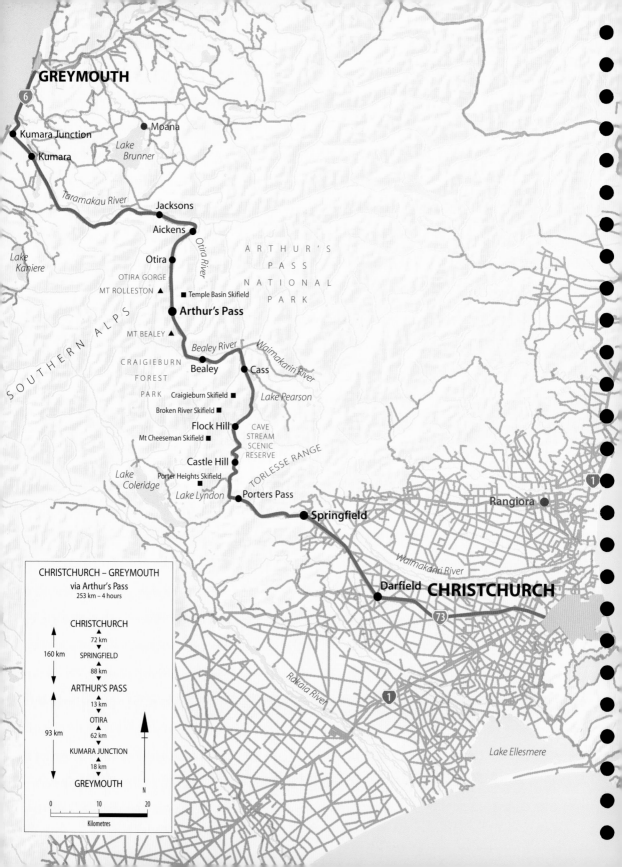

GREYMOUTH

⑥

Moana

Kumara Junction

Lake Brunner

Kumara

Taramakau River

Jacksons

Aickens

Lake Kaniere

Otira

Otira River

ARTHUR'S PASS NATIONAL PARK

OTIRA GORGE

MT ROLLESTON ▲   ■ Temple Basin Skifield

Arthur's Pass

MT BEALEY ▲

Bealey River   *Waimakariri River*

CRAIGIEBURN

FOREST   Bealey   Cass

Lake Pearson

PARK   ■ Craigieburn Skifield

■ Broken River Skifield

SOUTHERN ALPS

Flock Hill   CAVE
STREAM
SCENIC
RESERVE

Mt Cheeseman Skifield ■

Castle Hill   TORLESSE RANGE

*Lake
Coleridge*   Porter Heights Skifield ■

Lake Lyndon   Porters Pass

Springfield

Rangiora •

①

Springfield

Waimakariri River

Darfield   **CHRISTCHURCH**

⑦③

Rakaia River

①

Lake Ellesmere

CHRISTCHURCH – GREYMOUTH
via Arthur's Pass
253 km – 4 hours

▲
CHRISTCHURCH
▲
72 km
▼
160 km   SPRINGFIELD
▲
88 km
▼
ARTHUR'S PASS
▲
13 km
▼
93 km   OTIRA
▲
62 km
▼
KUMARA JUNCTION
▲
18 km
▼
GREYMOUTH

N

0   10   20

Kilometres

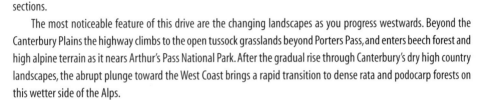

Christchurch–Greymouth via Arthur's Pass SH 73, 6
253 km, 4 hours

This superb route across the Southern Alps over Arthur's Pass was opened in 1866 – an astonishing feat given the rugged terrain early roadbuilders had to contend with, especially on the western approach up the Otira Valley. Even today there is a constant threat of rockfall, and the pass is regularly closed by snow in winter. But the completion of a viaduct from the Pass to the Otira River has eased the journey somewhat, and there are continued upgrades planned on the highway's difficult sections.

   The most noticeable feature of this drive are the changing landscapes as you progress westwards. Beyond the Canterbury Plains the highway climbs to the open tussock grasslands beyond Porters Pass, and enters beech forest and high alpine terrain as it nears Arthur's Pass National Park. After the gradual rise through Canterbury's dry high country landscapes, the abrupt plunge toward the West Coast brings a rapid transition to dense rata and podocarp forests on this wetter side of the Alps.

Springfield and the Canterbury Plains

Springfield (72 km from Christchurch) is the last of several small rural localities before the road climbs to Porters Pass. Springfield's tradition of hospitality dates to when horse-drawn Cobb & Co coaches travelled to and from the West Coast between 1866 and the 1920s. In keeping with this tradition, Springfield's Te Kowai Café serves up home-cooked food. Unfortunately for those who may have departed Christchurch early, a good coffee is hard to come by, even at the larger centre of Darfield which sports a couple of cafés.

Porters Pass (945 m) – walks, picnicking

Beyond Springfield the highway approaches the Torlesse Range which features the distinctive square-cut Torlesse Gap – according to local legend flying through the gap has exercised a few daredevil pilots. The range is a proposed conservation park which will protect the rare alpine flora and fauna known to exist there. SH 73 reaches Porters Pass and nearby Lake Lyndon at the southern end of the Torlesse range after a short haul from the plains. In winter this is a popular tobogganing and ski touring spot.

Castle Hill Scenic Reserve walks – picnicking

From Porters Pass the road sweeps towards Arthur's Pass along wide glaciated valleys. A few minutes drive from Porters is the turnoff to Porter Heights skifield, and shortly after on the left is Castle Hill Scenic Reserve – a weird landscape of limestone boulders favoured by rock climbers, botanists and walkers. Castle Hill village is a residential subdivision with no facilities for travellers. It is also a place revered by the West Coast's Waitaha tribe.

Cave Stream – walks, picnicking

Limestone boulder fields, scarps and vast unbroken scree fields dominate the vistas over the next few kilometres between Castle Hill, Flock Hill and Craigieburn Forest Park. At Cave Stream Scenic Reserve, up the hill from the Mt Cheeseman skifield turnoff, is a 'free caving' experience where in low flows it's possible to scramble through a limestone cave. Take a torch, wear strong shoes, dress for the wet and don't attempt it when the river is high, if it's raining or looking like rain.

Craigieburn Forest Park/Flock Hill – campground, walks, skiing

Beech forests arrive on the landscape at Craigieburn Forest Park where an unserviced camping area is located a few minutes from Cave Stream. Access roads lead to Broken River and Craigieburn skifields, then after a short winding section is Flock Hill Station (café and backpacker accommodation).

Flock Hill–Bealey – walks

Lake Pearson, home to a rare colony of crested grebe, is squeezed between hillsides and the long shifting screes on Purple Hill. Beyond here the route opens into space again toward Cass and the Waimakariri River. As the road edges past bluffs above the Waimakariri, horizons expand toward the Main Divide peaks, forests and tussock grasslands of Arthur's Pass. Just over Bruce Creek is a collection of holiday baches on Bealey Spur about a kilometre from the Bealey Hotel, where you can ask Paddy to tell you the one about the moa.

Arthur's Pass – walks, skiing

The highway enters the park at the Bealey Bridge over the Waimakariri. Klondyke Corner, the prominent forested corner on the opposite bank, has a camping ground and picnic area. Arthur's Pass village is located in the forested Bealey Valley 160 km from Christchurch. The park headquarters has information and excellent displays on the park's natural and human history. A Cobb & Co coach takes pride of place at the centre, which is a short distance from the railway tunnel (completed in 1923) that ended the era of horse-drawn transport over the pass. Of the short walks near the village, I would recommend the Devils Punchbowl Track (1.5 hours return).

From the village SH 73 enters the alpine zone as it winds up the Pass (920 m). There is a superb lookout up the Bealey Valley. Although Maori have been using the pass for centuries, the memorial near the highpoint is to the explorer Arthur Dudley Dobson who was the first European to cross it, in 1864. The view of Mt Rolleston from the steep Temple Basin skifield track (3 hours return) is one of the best in the park. A more sedate but rewarding short walk can be enjoyed in the Upper Otira Valley which is peppered with alpine flowers in summer. NB: This is an alpine region and walkers should be equipped for mountain weather.

The Devils Punchbowl Falls

Otira Gorge

The descent into the Otira rapidly brings you to a vastly different milieu of huge boulders, rainforest and a dark, foreboding valley which is leavened in summer by bright displays of rata. The painter Petrus van der Velden's bleak representations of the valley in the 1890s (one of which is hung at Christchurch's Robert McDougall Art Gallery) will seem familiar when you've been here in a storm. Below the gorge, Otira settlement is an untidy collection of railways-related buildings and a pub.

Upper Otira Valley

From Otira, the highway turns west at Aickens where the Otira River meets the wide and braided Taramakau. Like Springfield, Jacksons Hotel 18 km from Otira, has long been a travellers' rest. From Jacksons, Greymouth is 62 km away via Kumara Junction and SH 6, or about 75 km via Moana and Lake Brunner.

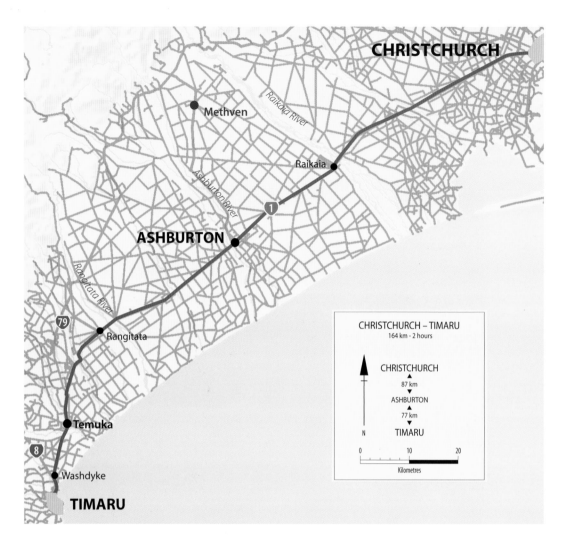

CHRISTCHURCH – TIMARU
164 km - 2 hours

N

CHRISTCHURCH
▲
87 km
▼
ASHBURTON
▲
77 km
▼
TIMARU

0   10   20
Kilometres

Christchurch–Dunedin SH 1
363 km, 5 hours

The drive south from Christchurch across the Canterbury Plains is a necessary chore that must be endured to reach routes to Mount Cook, the Waitaki Valley, Central Otago, Dunedin and further south to the Catlins.

Christchurch–Timaru
164 km, 2 hours

Ashburton
Ashburton is about 1 hour from Christchurch. Turn off at Ashburton along SH 77 to reach Methven and Mt Hutt skifield.

Timaru

Those intending to drive to Mount Cook can take SH 79 between Rangitata, Geraldine and Fairlie (see Woodend–Geraldine, Route 47). Alternatively, you can take the longer route along SH 8 from Washdyke, shortly before Timaru (just over 2 hours from Christchurch). Timaru hosts a regional port which exports timber, wool, meat and manufactures from South Canterbury.

Timaru–Dunedin

South of Timaru, SH 1 follows coastal plains to the Waitaki River and Oamaru. There is an excellent walkway at Otaio Beach near Otaio settlement. Thirty minutes from Timaru, just beyond Hook, SH 82 turns to Waimate township and up the north bank of the Waitaki River to Kurow (71 km from SH 1, see Omarama–Oamaru, Route 50).

Oamaru – campground, walks

Oamaru (3 hours from Christchurch) is world-renowned for its well-preserved collection of classical Victorian buildings made of 'Oamaru stone' (also called whitestone, a chalky limestone quarried in the district). Oamaru stone was used in the construction of many prominent Victorian-era buildings and churches in New Zealand, but nowhere else is it so well represented as an architectural feature – a fact celebrated at a festival each November. Oamaru is the childhood home of the novelist Janet Frame and setting for many of her early novels – a heritage trail allows walkers to visit sites that feature in those works. This and other trails, including the 'Ocean to Alps' trail up the Waitaki Valley, are covered by the *Heritage Trails of North Otago* booklet (free at information centres). Viewing blue penguins returning to their nests at dusk is another outstanding attraction – from a hide near the town centre.

Whitestone building, Oamaru

TIMARU – DUNEDIN
199 kms - 3 hours

TIMARU
▲
86 km
▼
OAMARU
▲
43 km
▼
MOERAKI
▲
28 km
▼
WAIKOUAITI
▲
42 km
▼
DUNEDIN

N

0   10   20
Kilometres

TIMARU
18/2/04

Otaio

Hook

Waimate

Waitaki River

82

1

OAMARU

Hampden
Moeraki   17/2/04
Moeraki Beach
Katiki

Shag River

SHAG POINT

Palmerston

Waikouaiti

Karitane

Seacliff

Warrington

Waitati

DUNEDIN

OTAGO
PENINSULA

8

Moeraki Boulders – campground, walks

These remarkable 60-million-year-old spherical 'concretions' are located on Moeraki Beach 43 km south of Oamaru, between Hampden and Moeraki village (campground). The boulders were formed in the Tertiary period by lime salts which accumulated around small objects on the seafloor. More recently they have fallen onto the beach from mudstone cliffs behind the beach. Maori folklore offers a less prosaic description – that they are petrified food baskets washed ashore from the great waka (canoe) Arai-te-Uru which capsized south of here at Shag Point. For many centuries Moeraki was the location of a large Maori settlement. The short walk along the beach to the boulders begins from a carpark signposted off the highway. Unfortunately the café here is a missed opportunity, but unless you are a café patron a donation is sought to cross the land to reach the boulders.

Shag Point

The association with Maori along this coast is continued as you drive south over a headland to Katiki Beach and Shag Point, once a stronghold of a Ngai Tahu hapu or sub-grouping. The reef off the mouth of the Shag River is said to be the upturned hull of the Arai-te-Uru canoe. A seal colony and sea lions are likely to be observed from the side road around the point towards the river mouth.

Moeraki boulders

Palmerston & Waikouaiti

A short distance from Shag Point is the village of Palmerston, (about 45 minutes from Dunedin). From here SH 1 traverses hill country to Waikouaiti, returning to the coast at Waitati (Blueskin Bay), before climbing over Kilmog Hill to Dunedin.

Karitane–Warrington coast route –swimming, views

A short but scenic diversion south of Waikouaiti is the coastal drive from Karitane to Warrington. Karitane is a popular beach resort and fishing settlement with a long and interesting history. It was first colonised by Maori and later by whalers, then the South Island's first mission station was established here as settlers established themselves in the nineteenth century. Given this history the small museum at Seacliff is an interesting place to visit. To many New Zealanders Karitane is associated with health reformer Sir Frederick Truby King who lived at Seacliff from 1889, founding the (still functioning) Plunket Society and 'Karitane' Hospitals to support mothers and babies.

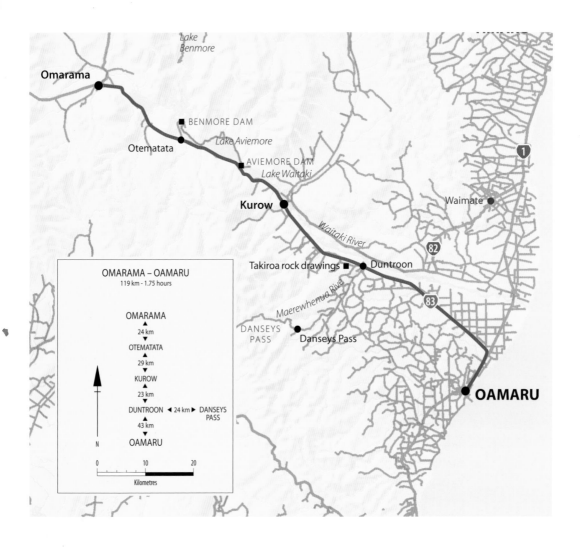

OMARAMA – OAMARU
119 km - 1.75 hours

OMARAMA
▲
24 km
▼
OTEMATATA
▲
29 km
▼
KUROW
▲
23 km
▼
DUNTROON ◄ 24 km ► DANSEYS
                          PASS
▲
43 km
▼
OAMARU

N

0   10   20
Kilometres

Omarama–Oamaru SH 83
119 km, 1.75 hours

The drive down the Waitaki River from Omarama is flanked by stark high country scenery and merino runs, but it's the artificial lakes of the Waitaki hydro scheme that dominate the landscape. The scheme produces one-third of New Zealand's electricity from eight power stations. Three hydro lakes – Benmore, Aviemore and Waitaki are on this route (the remaining five power stations are in the upper Waitaki. The drive is covered by the 'Ocean to the Alps' heritage trail in the *Heritage Trails of North Otago* booklet (free from information centres).

Otematata/Benmore dam – swimming, fishing, boating

The first lake on the Waitaki is Lake Benmore – this largest of the country's hydro storage lakes is retained by one of the largest earth dams in the Southern Hemisphere, completed in 1966. To reach Benmore dam turn off at Otematata – one of several villages built to house workers as the Waitaki was dammed. There is a visitor centre at the dam site which makes good use of displays to describe the workings of the Waitaki scheme and electricity generation to the North Island, but suffers from overzealous spin-doctoring about its environmental virtues. Tours are offered three times a day, at 11 a.m, and 1 and 3 p.m, daily in summer, weekends only in winter. From here you can drive across the dam and around the northern shores of Lake Aviemore, returning to SH 83 at Aviemore.

Aviemore and Waitaki dams

The Aviemore dam, 19 km from Otematata is an earth and concrete structure, completed in 1969. Lake Waitaki, smallest of the three hyrdo-lakes, filled the valley after the Waitaki dam was finished in 1934.

Kurow – campground

Kurow, with a population of about 411, is the largest centre in the valley. Many of its older buildings are constructed from Oamaru stone (see Oamaru above). From here the Waitaki River flows undammed to the sea: its trout and salmon fishing on the river are reputedly world class.

Takiroa Maori Rock Drawings

These well preserved charcoal and ochre rock drawings are found under a limestone overhang off the highway 3 km from Duntroon. While some drawings were unceremoniously chopped out of the wall and spirited to museums or private collections, the bulk remain. Interpretive panels describe the drawings and their origins.

Duntroon/Lower Waitaki – campground

Worth noting from Duntroon is the scenic route over Danseys Pass to Naseby and Ranfurly (SH 85, see also Dunedin–Cromwell via Middlemarch, Route 55). The route initially follows the Maerewhenua River to the Danseys Pass Holiday Park. Beyond here the road is unsealed and windy and should be driven carefully, if only to allow an appreciation of the wonderful tussock landscapes and schist outcrops on the pass. Not suitable for campervans. Allow 1.5 hours to Naseby.

Danseys Pass (photo Dave Chowdhury)

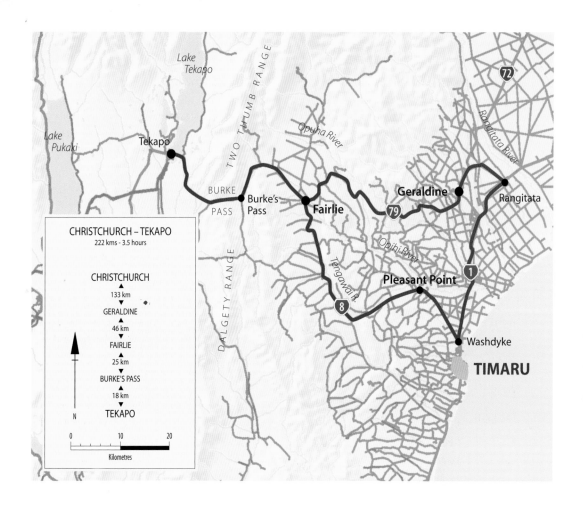

CHRISTCHURCH – TEKAPO
222 kms - 3.5 hours

CHRISTCHURCH
▲
133 km
▼
GERALDINE
▲
46 km
▼
FAIRLIE
▲
25 km
▼
BURKE'S PASS
▲
18 km
▼
TEKAPO

N

0   10   20
Kilometres

Christchurch–Wanaka SH 1, 79, 8
418 km, 6.5 hours

After climbing to the Mackenzie Basin from the Canterbury Plains, this drive traverses pictur-esque high country flanking the Southern Alps, past Aoraki/Mount Cook National Park and over Lindis Pass to Wanaka, base for excursions into Mount Aspiring National Park. These parks, moun-tain ranges and sequence of large glacial lakes are all part of the Te Wahipounamu South-West New Zealand World Heritage Area.

Christchurch–Tekapo, 222 km, 3.5 hours
From Christchurch take SH 1 south through Rakaia and Ashburton (see also Christchurch–Dunedin, Route 49). There are two routes to Fairlie from here. The first and quicker option is to leave SH 1 south of Rangitata and follow SH 79 to Fairlie via Geraldine (see Woodend–Geraldine, Route 47 for notes on Geraldine); the second is to continue to Washdyke and take SH 8 .

From Geraldine the route to Fairlie leaves the flatlands and wends its way through farmed hill country to reach a high point overlooking the Opuha Valley and the Two Thumb Range.

If driving from Washdyke, SH 8 to Fairlie allows easy travel up the Opihi and Tengawai valleys to Pleasant Point where the Pleasant Point steam railway operates in summer. The railway museum (at the station) doubles as an information centre. Pleasant Point has a great bakery, while the Opihi Winery Café is 20 minutes away near Hanging Rock.

Fairlie – campground

Fairlie styles itself as the 'gateway' to the Mackenzie Country, though really there's little at the town to recommend to travellers. Mackenzie was reputedly a 'wily' Scottish drover cum sheep rustler whose legendary exploits led to his name being permanently fixed to the area.

Burke Pass and the Mackenzie Basin

The actual gateway to the Mackenzie Country is 25 km west of Fairlie at Burke Pass where SH 8 slips between the Two Thumb and Dalgety ranges. Below the pass on the Fairlie side is Burke's Pass settlement with its tearooms and pub. A description of the pass as a 'portal' is very apt for here SH 8 enters the vast glaciated Mackenzie Basin, a region of lakes and undulating high country grasslands below the Southern Alps. Shortly beyond the pass is a lookout offering a first view of Aoraki/Mt Cook.

Lake Tekapo – campground, fishing

Tekapo is a holiday destination where scenic flights and the stone Church of the Good Shepherd on the lakeshore are especially popular with tourists. Lake Tekapo is the first of three large glacial lakes in the basin, all of which have been harnessed by the Waitaki power scheme (see notes on Omarama–Oamaru, Route 50). Canals traverse the basin linking lakes with power stations, and long lines of pylons take the energy generated away. While there's been considerable infrastructural development for the power scheme, ultimately it doesn't distract from the grandeur of the area's glacier-sculpted landscapes.

Tekapo–Wanaka, 196 km, 3 hours

The 47 km drive from Tekapo across the Mackenzie Basin past Lake Pukaki to the turnoff to Aoraki/Mount Cook National Park takes 30–40 minutes. Chances are though you'll stop often to appreciate the expansive and arresting lake/ grasslands/mountain vistas, even when clouds are pouring over the ranges during a nor'wester. An alternative route to Lake Pukaki is to drive along the Tekapo Canal to the Tekapo B power station on the eastern shore of Lake Pukaki – the canal drive begins about 13 km from Tekapo.

Aoraki/Mount Cook National Park – walks

Mount Cook Village is a 55 km (40-minute) drive along the western side of Lake Pukaki and the Tasman Valley. On a fine day this route offers stunning views of the national park's high peaks and glaciers including the country's highest mountain, Aoraki/Mt Cook (3755 m). Lake Pukaki fills the trench that formed when the Tasman Glacier retreated 10,000–13,000 years ago. The lake's level was artificially raised when the outlet was dammed for hydro-generation.

Aoraki/Mount Cook National Park is primarily an alpine climbing area, but there are a number of easy walks for the day visitor. Many of these, like the walks to Sealy Tarns or Blue Lakes on the Tasman

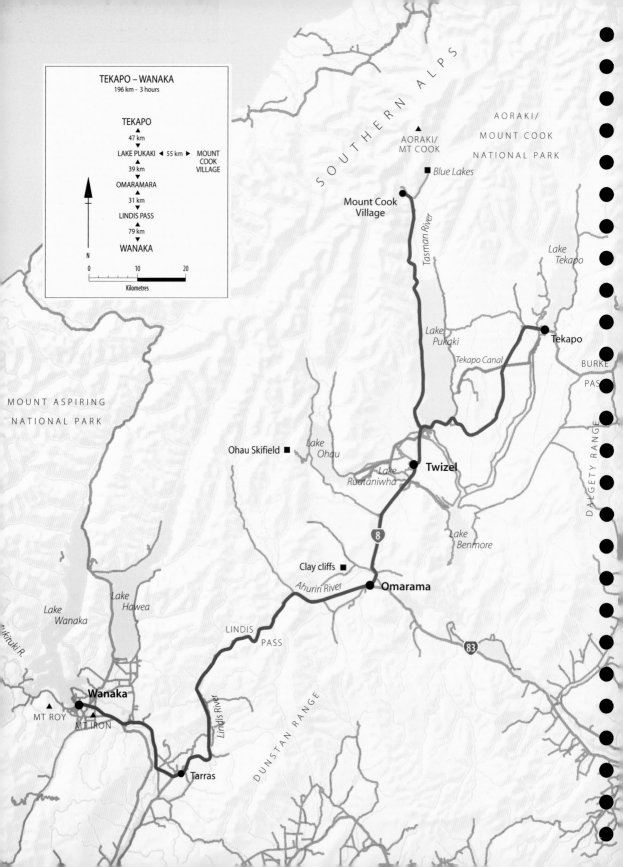

TEKAPO – WANAKA
196 km - 3 hours

TEKAPO
▲
47 km
▼
LAKE PUKAKI ◄ 55 km ► MOUNT
COOK
VILLAGE
▲
39 km
▼
OMARAMARA
▲
31 km
▼
LINDIS PASS
▲
79 km
▼
WANAKA

N

0   10   20
Kilometres

SOUTHERN ALPS

AORAKI/
MOUNT COOK
NATIONAL PARK

AORAKI/
MT COOK ▲

■ Blue Lakes

Mount Cook
Village ●

Tasman River

Lake
Pukaki

Lake
Tekapo

Tekapo ●

BURKE
PASS

Tekapo Canal

DALGETY RANGE

MOUNT ASPIRING

NATIONAL PARK

Ohau Skifield ■   Lake
Ohau

Lake
Ruataniwha

● Twizel

8

Lake
Benmore

Clay cliffs ■

Ahuriri River

● Omarama

83

LINDIS
PASS

Lake
Hawea

Lake
Wanaka

Lindis River

DUNSTAN RANGE

kiruki R.

Wanaka ●

MT ROY ▲   ▲
MT IRON

● Tarras

Glacier, lead to interesting glacial landforms and fine views. Information about the park is available at the park visitor centre and there's a reasonable café at the Hermitage Hotel. Rental car drivers should note that the Tasman Valley Road to the Tasman Glacier may be excluded from insurance cover – that said, the road is a straightforward drive as far as the Blue Lakes carpark.

Twizel – fishing

Twizel arose from the plains as a workers' village while the Waitaki power scheme was being constructed. It survives thanks to a steady tourism trade, the winter skiing industry based at the Ohau skifield, and New Zealanders who turned places vacated by redundant hydro workers into weekend holiday homes. Twizel is the base for a recovery programme for the critically endangered black stilt, a wading bird once common throughout New Zealand but now restricted to the braided rivers of the Mackenzie Basin. Guided tours of a captive rearing facility and viewing hide can be arranged from the Twizel Information Centre.

Lake Ohau & Clay Cliffs Reserve – walks, picnicking, fishing

From Twizel SH 8 continues south past Lake Ruataniwha. A side road 13 km from Twizel leads to the shores of Lake Ohau and to the Ohau skifield. Just before the Ahuriri River, prime black stilt habitat, signs indicate the way to the clay cliffs which are located on a side road above the Ahuriri River. Though on private land, this spectacular example of badland topography – deeply dissected ravines, pinnacles, gullies and sharp ridges eroded from gravels and silt – is protected by covenant, and is open to the public most of the year. Human connections with the cliffs area date to the earliest Polynesians who hunted moa and other birds from camps in the Waitaki Valley. Maori call the area Paritea, meaning white or light coloured cliff. A walking track leads into the heart of the cliffs area.

Omarama – fishing

Omarama has several tearooms, but the Clay Cliffs Estate Vineyard Café (500 m past Omarama, open from 11 a.m.) offers pleasant outdoor/indoor eating. Turn east from Omarama to reach SH 1 via the Waitaki Valley (SH 83, see Omarama–Oamaru, Route 50).

Lindis Pass (971 m)

The transition from the Canterbury high country into Central Otago's tawny tussock landscapes is made when SH 8 crosses Lindis Pass on the Dunstan Range. Much of the route over the pass occurs within Lindis Pass Scenic Reserve, which protects a large area of red-tussock grasslands. Over Lindis Pass SH 8 descends beside the Lindis River, a tributary of the Clutha. To reach Wanaka turn west on SH 8a just after Tarras.

Wanaka – campground, walks, fishing, skiing, boating

Wanaka is a sublime tourist town on the edge of Lake Wanaka, fourth largest lake in New Zealand. Drives around its southern shore and up the Matukituki Valley lead to Mount Aspiring National Park with fine views of Mt Aspiring. Walks in the Matukituki Valley, and (closer to Wanaka) to lookouts on Mt Roy (6 hours) and Mt Iron (45 minutes) offer spectacular views of the glaciated mountain scenery in this region. Of Wanaka's cafés, Kai Whaka Pai, on the lakefront, has few peers.

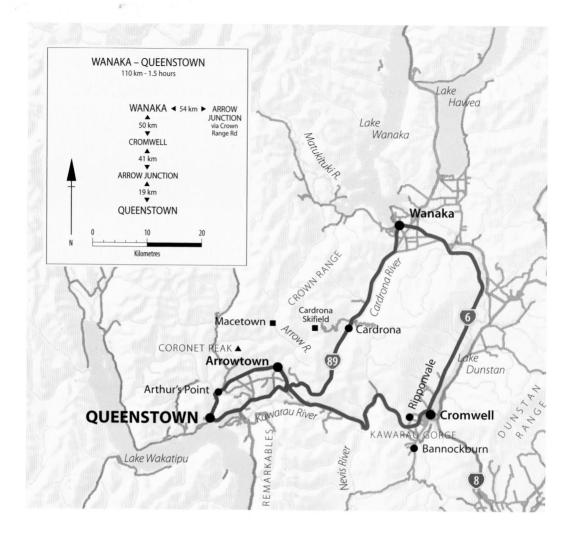

WANAKA – QUEENSTOWN
110 km - 1.5 hours

WANAKA ◄ 54 km ► ARROW
▲   JUNCTION
50 km   via Crown
▼   Range Rd
CROMWELL
▲
41 km
▼
ARROW JUNCTION
▲
19 km
▼
QUEENSTOWN

0   10   20
N
Kilometres

Wanaka–Queenstown

There are two routes between these centres, and each has its charms. The SH 6 route takes the traveller through wine and apricot-growing areas around Cromwell, and then through the Kawarau Gorge past historic mining sites and rugged Central Otago scenery. The Crown Range road is a scenic alpine route which reaches the greatest elevation of any public road in New Zealand.

Wanaka–Queenstown SH 6
110 km, 1.5 hours
From Wanaka drive to Cromwell (50 km) along the shores of Lake Dunstan. Close to Cromwell are the Bannockburn and Ripponvale wine-growing areas.

Kawarau Gorge

Twelve kilometres from Cromwell at the entrance to the Kawarau Gorge is the Goldfields Mining Centre, a working gold claim where visitors can pan for gold, view mining relics and machinery. Keeping high on its left bank, SH 6 follows the Kawarau River as it flows through the gorge's narrow defile below steep and overhanging walls of layered schist. Beyond the Nevis River confluence the route crosses the Kawarau and follows open terraces where several well-known Central Otago vineyards – including Gibbston Valley and Chard Farm – are located. Where the gorge narrows again is the famous A.J. Hackett bungy jumping operation off the historic Victoria Bridge. The Crown Range route from Wanaka meets SH 6 at Arrow Junction near Arrowtown.

Arrowtown – campground, walks, picnicking, swimming

Arrowtown is a picturesque holiday village, a short distance from SH 6, and 19 km from Queenstown. The area's colourful goldmining past is recreated at the town's museum, while walks towards Macetown reveal mining relics. There's pleasant swimming and picnicking by the Arrow River.

Crown Range Road
54 km (to SH 6 at Arrowtown), 1 hour

Now that the road is entirely sealed, this scenic traverse of the Crown Range offers a quick route to Queenstown. It travels south from Wanaka up the Cardrona Valley, past the historic Cardrona Hotel and the Cardrona Skifield. The climb through tussock landscapes to the crest of the Crown Range reaches 1121 m with spectacular views over Lake Wakatipu, The Remarkables and the area's glacial landforms. The descent toward Arrowtown is steep, culminating in a zigzag below Crown Terrace to SH 6.

Queenstown

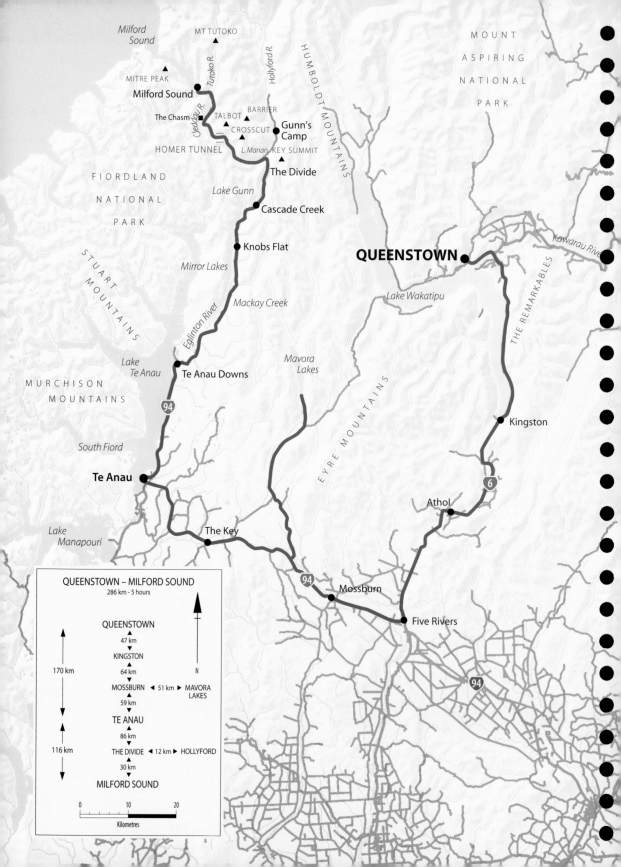

Milford Sound
MT TUTOKO ▲
Tutoko R.
▲ MITRE PEAK
Milford Sound ●
Cleddau R.
The Chasm ■
TALBOT ▲   BARRIER ▲
CROSSCUT ▲
Gunn's Camp ●
HOMER TUNNEL
L. Marian KEY SUMMIT
The Divide ●
Lake Gunn
Cascade Creek ●
Knobs Flat ●
Mirror Lakes
Mackay Creek
Eglinton River
Lake Te Anau
Te Anau Downs ●
94
South Fiord
Te Anau ●
Lake Manapouri
The Key ●
94
Mossburn ●

Hollyford R.
HUMBOLDT MOUNTAINS
MOUNT ASPIRING NATIONAL PARK
Kawarau River
QUEENSTOWN ●
THE REMARKABLES
Lake Wakatipu
Mavora Lakes
E Y R E   M O U N T A I N S
Kingston ●
6
Athol ●
Five Rivers ●
94

FIORDLAND NATIONAL PARK
STUART MOUNTAINS
MURCHISON MOUNTAINS

QUEENSTOWN – MILFORD SOUND
286 km - 5 hours

↑ N

QUEENSTOWN
47 km ▼
KINGSTON
64 km ▼
MOSSBURN ◄ 51 km ► MAVORA LAKES
59 km ▼
TE ANAU
86 km ▼
THE DIVIDE ◄ 12 km ► HOLLYFORD
30 km ▼
MILFORD SOUND

↕ 170 km
↕ 116 km

0   10   20
Kilometres

Queenstown–Milford Sound SH 6, 94
286 km, 5 hours

The 116 km Te Anau–Milford Highway in Fiordland National Park is undoubtedly one of the most rewarding drives in New Zealand. When it's fine the route combines spectacular mountain and forest scenery with some very good short walks and camping areas. In the wet, mountainsides become laced with waterfalls, and while driving may require more care, it is never dull. Fiordland incorporates almost half the 2.6 million ha Te Wahipounamu South-West New Zealand World Heritage Area, which recognises the outstanding natural and cultural features of this extraordinary landscape. For most tourists, Milford Sound is the 'must-visit' scenic icon of New Zealand, and because of that you must also put up with the worst aspects of mass tourism – crowds, tour buses, and noisy aircraft.

To reach Te Anau from Queenstown (3 hours) take SH 6 along the southern arm of Lake Wakatipu, past Kingston to Five Rivers. Here you turn off to Mossburn where SH 94 leads across undulating farmland to Te Anau. The drive around Lake Wakatipu is the most scenic part of this leg, with views to the Eyre Mountains. There are several lake-edge picnic sites near and at Kingston.

Athol
Were it not for the Lazybones Café, Athol, just under an hour from Queenstown, would be of little interest to travellers. But this is one excellent roadside eatery, and if leaving Queenstown early I'd recommend skipping that expensive Queenstown breakfast and heading straight to Athol to experience fine country cooking and mastery of the espresso machine.

Mavora Lakes – campground, walks, picnicking
The Mavora Lakes Park is 39 km along an easy unsealed road that leaves SH 94 about 12 km from Mossburn. It is a wonderful location, beech forested, and great for swimming, picnicking and fishing.

Beyond the Mavora Lakes' turnoff, SH 94 passes briefly through the Red Tussock Conservation Area, and from near The Key come first views of the Fiordland mountains.

Te Anau – campground, walks, picnicking
On the south-eastern shores of Lake Te Anau, this township is a very busy tourist centre in the summer months. The Fiordland National Park visitor centre is located near the eastern outskirts of the town, close to the DoC-run Te Anau Wildlife Centre where a number of native bird species can be viewed in aviaries. Among them are takahe, a critically endangered species whose only wild population is across Lake Te Anau in the Murchison Mountains. The Olive Tree Café on the main street has been a consistently good eatery over the years.

Milford Highway
If you're not rushing to catch a tour boat you can avoid choking on diesel fumes from the 90 or so tour buses that travel the highway daily (in summer), by leaving Te Anau around 2 p.m., when most are on the return journey. Without

stopping you can reach Milford Sound in about 2 hours, but you'd be missing plenty. DoC has published a good brochure on the history, natural features, short walks, campsites and other aspects of the highway. The sandflies are savage – repellent is a must for walkers and campers. Buy fuel at Te Anau – the return journey is within the range of most vehicles though fuel can be purchased (at great cost) at Milford or Gunn's Camp. In winter, the road may be closed by avalanches or snow.

The first leg of the journey to Milford is alongside Lake Te Anau, with views early on across the lake up the South Fiord and to the Stuart and Murchison mountains. Milford Track walkers need drive no further than Te Anau Downs, 30 minutes from Te Anau. From here the highway shifts inland past recovering stands of forest to the darker red beech forests of the Eglinton Valley.

Mackay Creek – campsites, walks, views, picnicking
The open grassy expanses of the river flats at Mackay Creek offer the first significant view of Fiordland's dramatic landscapes, which like the rest of the Southern Alps were carved by vast glaciers. What's different is that the erosion-resistant qualities of Fiordland's granite, gneiss and diorite rocks have preserved the glacial imprint in its steep walls, summits and U-shaped valleys – when elsewhere in the South Island softer rocks have given way to a less angular topography.

Mirror Lakes – campsites, walks, views
A five minute boardwalk excursion to a valley-edge wetland, with clear pools containing trout and waterfowl (including scaup, mallard and shags). Forest birds flit through red and silver beech forest, from common tomtits and fantails to the rare rifleman.

Knobs Flat – shelter, campsite
A public shelter here has panels describing the road's history, the work of avalanche controllers, natural history and the world heritage area.

Lake Gunn
The 45-minute Lake Gunn nature walk (76 km from Te Anau) is accessible to wheelchairs.

The Divide – shelter, walks
The Divide is the forest pass separating the Eglinton and Hollyford valleys. It is the start/finish point for the Routeburn and Greenstone tracks, as well as the popular walk to Key Summit (3 hours return), a subalpine wetland offering outstanding views of Fiordland and north towards Mount Aspiring National Park. From the Divide, SH 94 enters the most spectacular section of the highway, beginning with the steep descent to the Hollyford River. 'Pops View' is a well-situated lookout with vistas east to the Humboldt Mountains, and west towards the U-shaped hanging valley of Marian Creek below Mt Crosscut.

Hollyford Valley – campground, walks
The Hollyford Rd (unsealed) branches off northwards at the base of the descent. A 10-minute forest walk along the Lake Marian track, about a kilometre from the junction, crosses the Hollyford to reach a spec-

tacular cataract. Gunn's Camp, 8 km from the junction, features a campground, store, a great little museum, and the droll humour of camp-owner Mr Murray Gunn.

From the junction SH 94 climbs the steep fall of the Hollyford River to the subalpine grass and shrublands of the upper Hollyford Valley. Near the Homer Tunnel, the prominent pyramid of Mt Talbot overlooks boulder fields and vegetation decimated by winter and spring avalanches. On the right, up the Gertrude Valley, is the aptly named Mt Barrier.

Homer Tunnel & Cleddau Valley – walks
Homer Tunnel, constructed between 1934 and 1954, bores through Homer Saddle to the Cleddau Valley. At the carpark at the Hollyford end you'll quite likely encounter inquisitive kea, a mountain parrot, but please observe the entreaty not to feed them. At the tunnel's western end the road emerges into the breathtaking Cleddau Valley and starts a winding descent to the Cleddau River. In a storm the sight of waterfalls cascading thousands of metres down the bluffs is unforgettable.

The short walk to The Chasm takes you to where the Cleddau River is forced through a slot gorge. As you descend through forests toward Milford Sound there are occasional sightings of snowcapped Mt Tutoko (2746 m), the highest peak in Fiordland – best viewed from the Tutoko River bridge. Just past the Donne River are first views of Mitre Peak.

Milford Sound – campground, walks, boat tours
It's not possible for the overexposure of Mitre Peak and Milford Sound in countless brochures, posters and tourist department advertisements to take anything away from your first sight of them. Milford is busy and noisy, but if you can stay longer than an hour, you'll find a moment of quiet and perhaps some solitude on a walk to appreciate how wonderful the place is.

The best place for lunch or a meal is at Milford Sound 'Lodge', a backpacker hostel and campground located a kilometre back up the road.

Mitre Peak, Milford Sound

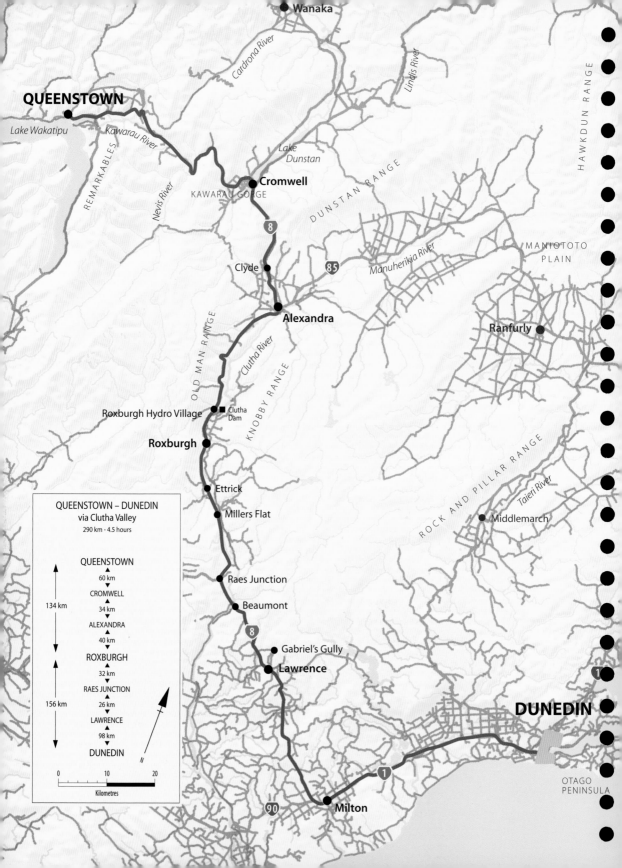

Wanaka

Cardrona River

Lindis River

H A W K D U N   R A N G E

QUEENSTOWN

Lake Wakatipu

Kawarau River

R E M A R K A B L E S

Nevis River

Lake Dunstan

KAWARAU GORGE

Cromwell

D U N S T A N   R A N G E

(8)

(85)

Manuherikia River

M A N I O T O T O
P L A I N

Clyde

Alexandra

Ranfurly

Clutha River

O L D   M A N   R A N G E

K N O B B Y   R A N G E

R O C K   A N D   P I L L A R   R A N G E

Taieri River

Roxburgh Hydro Village   ■ Clutha Dam

Roxburgh

Ettrick

Middlemarch

Millers Flat

Raes Junction

Beaumont

(8)

Gabriel's Gully

Lawrence

DUNEDIN

(1)

OTAGO
PENINSULA

(90)   (1)   **Milton**

N

QUEENSTOWN – DUNEDIN
via Clutha Valley
290 km - 4.5 hours

QUEENSTOWN
▲
60 km
CROMWELL
▲
134 km   34 km
ALEXANDRA
▲
40 km
ROXBURGH
▲
32 km
RAES JUNCTION
▲
156 km   26 km
LAWRENCE
▲
98 km
DUNEDIN

0   10   20
Kilometres

Queenstown–Dunedin via Clutha Valley SH 8
290 km, 4.5 hours

Queenstown to Alexandra (94 km) is a scenic 1.5 hour drive through the Kawarau Gorge to Cromwell and along the shores of Lake Dunstan (this leg of the route is described in the Wanaka–Queenstown, Route 52 and Cromwell–Dunedin, Route 55 sections).

From Alexandra, SH 8 travels south along the Clutha Valley, renowned for its orchards, brown trout and quinnat salmon fishing, and jet boating on the Clutha River. Between Alexandra and Roxburgh the route tracks through a distinctive Central Otago landscape, flanked on the west by the Old Man Range and on the east by the Knobby Range. There are expansive views over the Clutha, undulating grasslands and outcrops of schist. Fruitlands Gallery Café is located shortly before the road descends to Roxburgh Hydro Village.

Roxburgh – campground
Lake Roxburgh was formed when the Clutha was dammed near Roxburgh in the early 1950s – at one stage this was the largest dam in New Zealand (the largest now is Benmore in the Waitaki Valley). Near the dam Lake Roxburgh Lodge offers lunch for passing travellers. Roxburgh township, 40 km from Alexandra, is the centre of the valley's pipfruit growing industry. Roxburgh's famous red apricot is said to have been first planted in 1866 by a local who bought a tree off a passing swagger. Tours of Roxburgh's orchards and gardens are a popular activity and there is a museum situated in a former Methodist Church (1872).

Roxburgh–Lawrence
SH 8 continues southwards through Ettrick and Millers Flat, before crossing the Clutha at Beaumont. The Seed Farm just before Ettrick offers lunches and Devonshire teas, and there are roadside fruit stalls in Ettrick itself. At Raes Junction, 72 km from Alexandra, SH 90 turns off to Gore (67 km).

Lawrence
Lawrence etched its place in New Zealand history when gold was struck in nearby Gabriel's Gully in May 1861 – a discovery that helped lift New Zealand out of economic depression. This famous strike saw 11,000 diggers arrive within two months – twice the then population of Dunedin. In 1862, 5670 kg of gold was extracted from the area, but pro-

Schist outcrop, Central Otago

duction declined thereafter. Lawrence is a quieter place these days, the centre of a prosperous wool-growing industry. SH 1 is met 37 km from Lawrence, just south of Milton, and 50 minutes (61 km) drive from Dunedin.

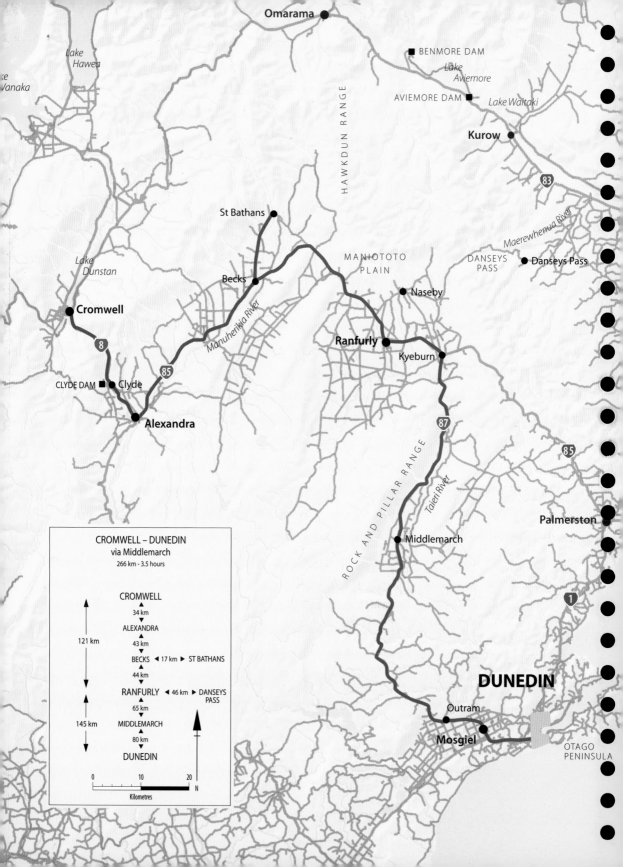

Omarama

BENMORE DAM

Lake Hawea

Lake Aviemore

AVIEMORE DAM   *Lake Waitaki*

Kurow

HAWKDUN RANGE

83

Maerewhenua River

St Bathans

MANIOTOTO PLAIN

DANSEYS PASS   Danseys Pass

Lake Dunstan

Becks

Naseby

Cromwell

8

Manuherikia River

Ranfurly

Kyeburn

85

85

CLYDE DAM   Clyde

Alexandra

87

Taieri River

ROCK AND PILLAR RANGE

Palmerston

Middlemarch

1

CROMWELL – DUNEDIN
via Middlemarch
266 km - 3.5 hours

CROMWELL
▲
34 km
▼
ALEXANDRA
▲
43 km
▼
BECKS ◄ 17 km ► ST BATHANS
▲
44 km
▼
RANFURLY ◄ 46 km ► DANSEYS PASS
▲
65 km
▼
MIDDLEMARCH
▲
80 km
▼
DUNEDIN

121 km

145 km

0   10   20
Kilometres
N

DUNEDIN

Outram

Mosgiel

OTAGO PENINSULA

Cromwell–Dunedin via Middlemarch SH 8, 85, 87
266 km, 3.5 hours

This route traverses Central Otago where wide undulating valleys float between dun-coloured ranges – landscapes almost made mythical by the painter Grahame Sydney and the makers of car and beer ads.

Clyde/Alexandra – campground

From Cromwell it's a 20-minute drive around Lake Dunstan to Clyde and Alexandra. Politics of the controversial Clyde dam aside, Clyde has shaken its recent hydro-town past and reverted to sleepy holidaysville with several cafés and a bakery, historical museums proclaiming its goldmining history, and old stone buildings made straight out of the schist landscape. All of which neatly complements nearby Alexandra's wine and historical trails and roadside stalls selling orchard-grown apricots and other stone fruits for which the area is famous.

St Bathans – walks, picnicking

Up the Manuherikia Valley SH 85 travels by sheep-runs and localities with little more than a pub to their name. The valley is wide, the hills gentle, and the air so clear that climate scientists live in Lauder to study the atmosphere. Historic St Bathans, 17 km off the highway (sealed) from Becks, is one of the best preserved sites in the Otago Goldfields Park. The town's collection of nineteenth century wooden, stone and mudbrick buildings stands on the edge of disused goldworkings that date to the 1860s gold rush. The rustic mudbrick Vulcan Hotel (1882) and the Post Office (1909) are still open for business.

Ranfurly/Naseby

From Becks, SH 85 rounds Ragged Ridge and North Rough Ridge and enters the expansive tussock grasslands of the Maniototo Plain beneath the Hawkdun Range. Ranfurly has reinvented itself as a centre for rural art deco and now has an art deco festival in February each year. There's also an interesting railway station museum. Naseby, 14 km north of Ranfurly near the Naseby pine plantation, is a lovely village with period buildings, craft shops and a village green. The historic Danseys Pass Hotel and Kyeburn Gold Diggings is 20 minutes from here along a rough unsealed road. If travelling to Palmerston (SH 1), allow 45 minutes from Ranfurly.

Middlemarch – walks

Just past Kyeburn turn south onto SH 87 for the 129 km/1.5 hour drive through Middlemarch to Mosgiel and Dunedin. Flanked by the Rock and Pillar Range, SH 87 follows the meandering Taieri River and the Central Otago Rail Trail – the old railway route now developed into a historic walking track and mountain bike trail. Beyond Middlemarch the highway climbs through rolling hills, offering fine views back to the Maniototo before it descends to Outram and Mosgiel to join SH 1.

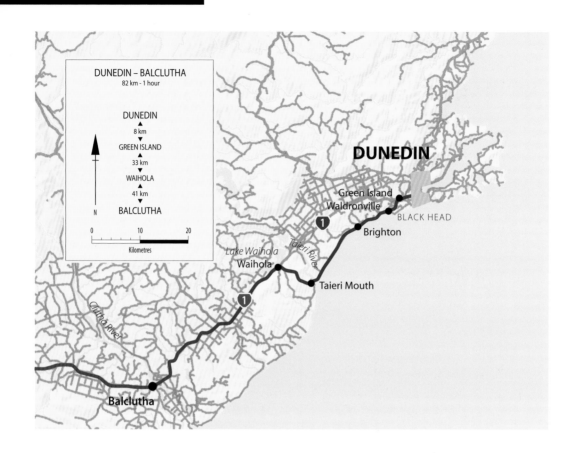

DUNEDIN – BALCLUTHA
82 km - 1 hour

DUNEDIN
▲
8 km
▼
GREEN ISLAND
▲
33 km
▼
WAIHOLA
▲
41 km
▼
BALCLUTHA

N

0   10   20
Kilometres

DUNEDIN

Green Island
Waldronville
BLACK HEAD
Brighton
Lake Waihola
Taieri River
Waihola
Taieri Mouth
Clutha River
Balclutha

Dunedin–Invercargill SH 1
219 km, 3 hours

Dunedin–Taieri Mouth–Lake Waihola

The quickest route from Dunedin to Invercargill is by SH 1 across the Taieri Plains, but promoters of the 'Southern Scenic Route' also direct travellers along the coast south of Dunedin as far as Taieri Mouth. To reach the coast, turn off at Green Island just west of the city and make for Waldronville. Black Head is an impressive basalt cliff east of Waldronville — well worth the few extra minutes required to divert there. The route passes through the beach resort of Brighton and follows the rocky coastline to Taieri Mouth. Here it turns inland (unsealed) to Lake Waihola where it rejoins SH 1. Walks up to 4 hours can be made in the Taieri River gorge. Camping and picnicking sites are located at Taieri Mouth and Brighton. Lake Waihola is a popular recreation area, and birdwatchers will enjoy a visit to the Sinclair Wetlands near here.

Balclutha – campground

From Balclutha, SH 1 heads west toward Clinton and Gore through the rolling country landscape made prosperous by Southland's wool growers. The stretch between Clinton and Gore was declared the 'Presi-

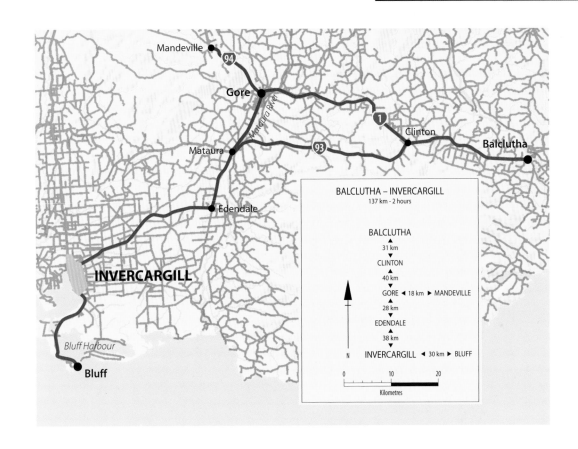

dential Highway' when President Clinton visited New Zealand in 1999. From Clinton, SH 93 offers a by-pass to Mataura (1 hour).

Gore – campground
Gore is a pleasant town on the banks of the Mataura River, a renowned brown trout fishery. The modern, well-designed Hokonui Moonshine Museum is a must-stop attraction that recounts Gore's colourful history as the centre of an illicit trade moonshining whisky during the area's 'dry' years. You can sample some moonshine, or buy a bottle of it, but pester the barman for the location of the still at your peril: 'I could tell ya, but then I'd have to kill ya'. Over the road, Gore's Eastern Southland Gallery will feature, from late 2001, a number of works by Rita Angus and Ralph Hotere in its permanent display. Ten minutes from Gore on SH 94, Croydon Air Services welcomes casual visitors to its vintage aircraft restoration workshop at Mandeville Airfield – Tiger Moths are a speciality, as are joyride flights.

From Gore, Invercargill is about 40 minutes via Mataura and Edendale. Bluff, at the end of SH 1 is 20 minutes from Invercargill.

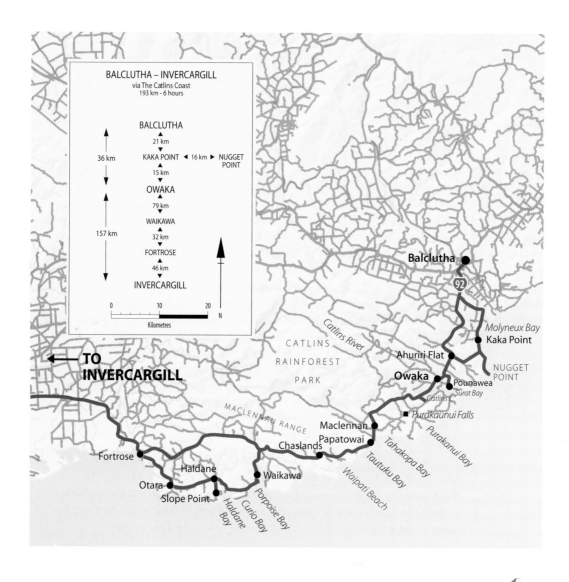

BALCLUTHA – INVERCARGILL
via The Catlins Coast
193 km - 6 hours

BALCLUTHA
▲
21 km
▼
KAKA POINT ◄ 16 km ► NUGGET POINT
▲
15 km
▼
OWAKA
▲
79 km
▼
WAIKAWA
▲
32 km
▼
FORTROSE
▲
46 km
▼
INVERCARGILL

36 km

157 km

0   10   20
Kilometres

N

TO INVERCARGILL ←

Balclutha

92

CATLINS RAINFOREST PARK

Catlins River

Molyneux Bay
Kaka Point
Ahuriri Flat
NUGGET POINT
Owaka
Pounawea
Surat Bay
Catlins L.
Purakaunui Falls
Purakanui Bay
Tahakopa Bay
Tautuku Bay
Waipati Beach

MACLENNAN RANGE

Maclennan
Papatowai
Chaslands

Fortrose
Haldane
Waikawa
Otara
Slope Point
Porpoise Bay
Curio Bay
Haldane Bay

Balclutha–Invercargill via the Catlins Coast SH 92
193 km (approximately), 6 hours

The southeast corner of the South Island is a remarkably beautiful area renowned for its coastal forests, wildlife, beaches and scenery. Mercifully, the Catlins hasn't yet been subjected to excessive tourism development. What services there are for tourists — the campgrounds, backpackers, homestays and specialist 'eco-tourism' operations are small-scale and low impact, and this feels right for the area. Tourists and providers of small-scale accommodation cottoned on to the potential of the Catlins long before local tourism planners — so much so that the Southern Scenic Route, the premiere touring route through the Catlins still has a lengthy section that is unsealed, as are most of the side routes to the coast and link roads. Even more bizarrely, the official route bypasses some of the Catlins' most scenic locations. This being the case it requires map-reading and careful driving on gravel roads to experience the best from a visit here.

Kaka Point/Nugget Point – campground, walks, views

From Balclutha drive south on SH 92 and take the turnoff 6 km from Balclutha to Kaka Point village (15 km from turnoff) on the edge of Molyneux Bay where there is a pleasant beach, store and kids' playground. From here it's an increasingly spectacular 16 km drive around the coast to Nugget Point. Nugget Point lighthouse, built in 1869, is an airy but quite safe five minute walk from the carpark. In residence on the rocky platform below the beacon on my turn here were fur and elephant seals, Hookers sea lions, and blue and yellow-eyed penguins. Back toward Kaka Point a track leads to the Roaring Bay viewing hides, best used at dusk when penguins are coming ashore.

Nugget Point

Owaka, Pounawea and Surat Bay – campground, walks, swimming

To reach Owaka from Kaka Point, take the gravel road from Willsher Bay to SH 92 at Ahuriri Flat. Owaka (15 km from Kaka Point) is the largest settlement in the Catlins so has most services tourists require. The Lumberjack Café was in February 2001 the only place between Balclutha and Invercargill offering something that resembled a good coffee.

To get to Pounawea and Surat Bay turn east at Owaka. Both are on the shores of the Catlins River estuary. There's a campground and safe swimming at Pounawea, while at Surat Bay near the Catlins Heads, Hookers sea lions are often encountered lounging on the inner beach during summer (while rarely known to have a go at humans, it still pays to give them a wide berth). The beach walk from Surat Bay backpacker lodge to the outer coast is a highlight, particularly when the sea lions are about.

Purakaunui Falls/Purakaunui Bay – campground, walks, picnicking

Just past Catlins Lake (the head of the Catlins River estuary), leave SH 92 again and take the signposted road to Purakaunui Falls. The tarmac soon ends as the road winds toward the remnant beech forest containing the track to the falls (20 minutes return). Before the falls a road leads to Purakaunui Bay where there is a lovely beach with camping and picnicking areas.

Tahakopa Bay/Papatowai – campground, walks

From the Purakaunui Falls carpark, take the left fork and continue along the unsealed route to Maclennan on the edge of the Catlins Coastal Rainforest Park. At the bridge over the forest fringed estuary formed by the Tahakopa River is a carpark and the start of the 'Old Coach Rd' walk. This is an easy forest walk (80 minutes return) to the river mouth and Tahakopa Bay, the site of an early Polynesian moa-hunter camp.

Over the bridge, Papatowai is a small holiday settlement with a pleasant beach-side picnicking spot beneath the totara trees at Picnic Point, and opportunity for long beach walks. On Cross St (up the hill from the beach access) is the 35-minute Picnic Point forest walk. Papatowai once supported a considerable Maori population in pre-European times – from the bones that have been unearthed here it's thought this was one of the last moa habitats in New Zealand.

Tautuku Bay – walks, swimming

The tarmac ends just beyond Papatowai and isn't regained for another 25 km. Be wary of truckies and others who travel this road at speed. From Papatowai there's a dusty 2 km climb up Florence Hill to the wonderful viewpoint overlooking Tautuku Beach, Tautuku Peninsula and forest from the coast to the Maclennan Range – welcome respite from the sparseness of the farmed landscape encountered on much of the drive thus far.

The turnoff to Tautuku beach is not far down the hill. As well as the beach there are two quality walks from the road worth considering: Lake Wilkie, a 20-minute forest walk; and the Tautuku estuary boardwalk (also 20 minutes).

Cathedral Caves – walk

Beyond Tautuku Bay, the road crosses a forested range in the Tautuku Scenic Reserve in which rimu, kamahi and roadside groves of fuchsia are striking features. Twelve kilometres from Papatowai is the access to Cathedral Caves at Waipati Beach. The access track crosses private land and is opened only when tides allow. There is a small charge for crossing the land, well worth it for the 25-minute walk to these beautiful limestone caves. Ask at information centres for access details.

Waikawa/Curio Bay – campground, walks, swimming

The tarmac is regained soon after the road crosses Chaslands, a farmed area entirely surrounded by forest. The T-junction at the conclusion of the forest portion of this drive offers the choice of continuing west along the Southern Scenic Route to Invercargill (80 km), or the more interesting option of heading south to Waikawa, Curio Bay and the coastal route to Fortrose.

Waikawa, 6 km from the junction, has a small café cum information centre and museum. By now the tarmac will have been extended the next 7 km to Curio Bay, the settlement on the shores of Porpoise Bay famous for its surf beach, rare Hector's dolphins, yellow-eyed and blue penguins, seals and the nearby fossil forest.

The 20 or so Hector's dolphins resident in Porpoise Bay are a delight. Being inshore feeders they will often be seen in the surf – this is the only place in the country where dolphins venture so close in. Given the small size of the group here, and because the species overall is so perilously close to extinction, humans must make a special effort not to disturb these creatures. Indeed, the guidebooks that have promoted the bay as a place to swim with dolphins have caused much alarm here. DoC's guidelines stipulate that Hector's dolphins shouldn't be fed, touched or approached (they will move toward you if they want to). Lastly, don't enter the water within 50 m of a dolphin.

The 180 million year old fossilised forest exposed on the outgoing tide at Curio Bay is another of the area's internationally significant marvels. This is part of one of the largest and least-disturbed Jurassic-era fossil forests in the world – stumps, entire trunks and root systems can be discerned in the rock platform and cliffs. The story of the forest is recounted on the information panel at the bay.

Slope Point – walk

From Curio Bay the travel is again on unsealed roads for approximately 15 km towards Otara. Below another large remnant of forest, the route skirts a dune lake and the tidal estuary inland of Haldane Bay, and eventually reaches a T-junction at Haldane. From here you can make a brief 5 km diversion toward Slope Point, the most southerly point of the South Island. Even if you don't make the 20-minute walk across farmland to the Point (closed in September and October) the drive offers fine views of the coast, Foveaux Strait and Stewart Island. The Southern Scenic Route is joined again at Fortrose, northwest of Otara and 46 km from Invercargill.

Tautuku Beach, Catlins (photo Dave Chowdhury)

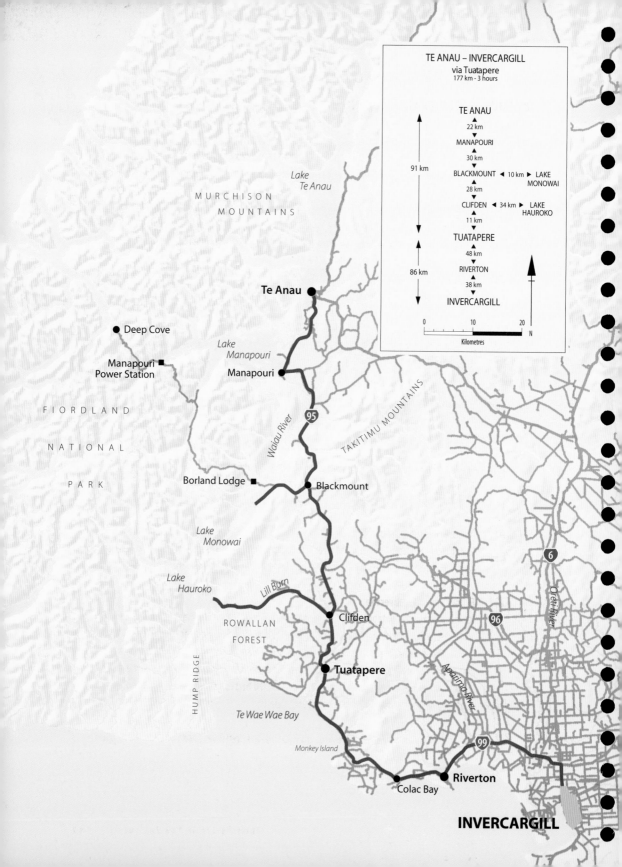

TE ANAU – INVERCARGILL
via Tuatapere
177 km - 3 hours

TE ANAU
22 km
MANAPOURI
30 km
BLACKMOUNT ◄ 10 km ► LAKE MONOWAI
28 km
CLIFDEN ◄ 34 km ► LAKE HAUROKO
11 km
TUATAPERE
48 km
RIVERTON
38 km
INVERCARGILL

91 km

86 km

0   10   20
Kilometres

N

Te Anau

Deep Cove

Manapouri
Power Station

Lake
Te Anau

MURCHISON
MOUNTAINS

Lake
Manapouri

Manapouri

Waiau River

95

TAKITIMU MOUNTAINS

FIORDLAND

NATIONAL

PARK

Borland Lodge

Blackmount

Lake
Monowai

Lake
Hauroko

Lill Burn

6

Clifden

ROWALLAN

FOREST

96

Oreti River

Tuatapere

HUMP RIDGE

Te Wae Wae Bay

Aparima River

Monkey Island

99

Colac Bay

Riverton

INVERCARGILL

Te Anau–Invercargill via Tuatapere SH 95, 99
177 km, 3 hours

This route (the western leg of Southland's 'Southern Scenic Route') follows the forested eastern edge of Fiordland down the Waiau Valley to Te Wae Wae Bay. Scenic highlights are the beautiful glacier-formed lakes: Manapouri, Monowai and Hauroko.

Manapouri –campground, walks, swimming, fishing
Manapouri, on the edge of Lake Manapouri 22 km from Te Anau, is part tourist centre, hydro village and holiday home location. Although its lake, forest and mountain scenery is no less stunning than Te Anau, Manapouri has the virtue of being a far quieter place. Most come here to make the lake cruise to the Manapouri Power Station and the spectacular tour from the station to Deep Cove.

Lake Monowai – campground, picnicking, fishing
The next leg follows the Waiau River as it meanders between Fiordland National Park and the Takitimu Mountains. Lake Monowai is accessed from Borland Rd approximately 30 km from Manapouri. The lake is 10 km from the intersection along an easy unsealed road (NB: driving beyond Borland Lodge is not recommended as the road is narrow and poorly maintained).

Lake Hauroko – campground, picnicking, swimming, fishing
Back on the Southern Scenic Route, continue down the Waiau Valley 28 km to Clifden, site of a beautiful suspension bridge over the Waiau, opened in 1899. The 34 km side trip up the Lill Burn to Lake Hauroko begins 500 m from the bridge. The road is unsealed but in good condition; the last few kilometres to the lake is through forest. A short forest loop in the Dean Forest leads to a huge 1000-year-old totara.

Tuatapere – campground
Tuatapere, 11 km from Clifden, is the base for exploring the western reaches of the Te Wae Wae Bay coast, Rowallan Forest and multi-day tramps around Fiordland's south coast and the Hump Ridge.

Te Wae Wae Bay–Riverton
Ten kilometres from Tuatapere, SH 99 reaches the magnificent Te Wae Wae Bay. Between here and Riverton are several places of interest, notably McCrackens Rest (views of the bay, information on the area's natural, Maori and European history); Monkey Island, at the eastern end of the bay (sacred to Maori, site of a gold rush tent town, safe swimming, picnicking); Cosy Nook (a delightful fishing settlement); Colac Bay (excellent beach and campground). Last but not least, the best coffee between Te Anau and Invercargill is made at Riverton's superbly located Beachfront Café.

From Riverton, allow 25 minutes to cross the Aparima and Oreti River floodplains to Invercargill.

INDEX

INDEX